NO PLACE LIKE HOME
ECHOES FROM KOSOVO

NO PLACE LIKE HOME
ECHOES FROM KOSOVO

MELANIE FRIEND

midnight
editions

Published in the United States by Midnight Editions, an imprint of Cleis Press Inc., P.O. Box 14684, San Francisco, California 94114.
Printed in Singapore.
Cover design: Scott Idleman
Text design: Bernie Schimbke
First Edition
10 9 8 7 6 5 4 3 2 1

Library of Congress Cataloging-on-Publication Data
Friend, Melanie, 1957-
No place like home : echoes from Kosovo / Melanie Friend.-- 1st ed.
        p. cm.
ISBN: 1-57344-119-8 (alk. Paper)
1. Kosovo (Serbia)--History--Personal narratives, Albanian. I. Title: Echoes from Kosovo. II. Title.
DR2087.7.F75 2001
949.7103--dc21
2001032399

A catalog record is available from the British Library.

MIDNIGHT EDITIONS is a new publishing venture whose mission is to enlarge our understanding of human rights by publishing works from regions where repression and censorship endanger creative expression. We publish and promote the work of journalists, creative writers and photographers, engaged in the complex art of reporting and documenting history. We welcome your comments. Please contact us: www.midnighteditions.com

For my friends in Kosovo/a

CONTENTS

ACKNOWLEDGMENTS

I would like to thank Rrahman and Melihate Dedaj, Mehmet and Miradije Aliu, and Rachel Wareham for all their warm hospitality over the years.

Many thanks to all the interpreters who worked with me, particularly Edita Arifi, who interpreted for many of the interviews and accompanied me to Reçak and Celinë, and Rresearta Reka, who accompanied me to Lubizhde. Many thanks to Rema Asllani, Cuca Fetahu, Antigona Mustafa-Kaçamaku, Ilmie Rexha and Diar Sinani. Among the interpreters who did not wish to give their surnames, I would particularly like to thank Islam, Dijana, Mira, Slaviša, and Mila, who translated at Gračko. Thanks to Abdurahim Sulejmani and Fexhri Xheladini in Macedonia for all their help over the years. Special thanks to Semih Bülbül of UNHCR Prizren office and to Igballe Rogova of Motrat Qiriazi.

Many thanks to drivers Azemine Aliu and Jeton Aliu for working long hours over hazardous roads and miraculously avoiding any accidents...

I am grateful for access arranged by Swedish KFOR (Gunnar Wahlin and Marko Wramen), Finnish KFOR (Mikko Niiles), Polish KFOR (particularly Andrzej Dylong for expert driving up to Koshtanjeve!), British KFOR (Allan Youp), the Royal Marines and the Royal Regiment of Fuseliers (Neil Wright), Ukrainian KFOR (Dmitry Shkurko) and UNMIK police.

I'm grateful to the following for information: Amnesty International, Human Rights Watch, ICRC, ICTY, IWPR, Kosova Information Centre, Minority Rights Group, OSCE, UNHCR, UNMIK Prizren, Cynthia Cockburn, and Dr. Donald Kenrick.

Special thanks to Adrian Foreman in London for advice on the manuscript, and to Miranda Vickers and Bob Churcher of International Crisis Group for invaluable help. Also many thanks to Neil Finer.

A big thank you to Arta Dedaj in London (particularly for her endless patience with spellings), Vlora Dedaj, Fadil Alija, Sabrina Budalica, and Sanja Thompson.

Warm thanks to Liz Jobey, for early encouragement, and to friends who helped with picture editing or as readers—Crispin Hughes, Caroline Penn, Brenda Prince, Alison Read, Emma Sandon and especially Maggie Murray. Thanks to Carol-Ann Allen for her great advice and support. Thanks to John Watkins, who, in 1992, encouraged me to report about Kosovo for BBC radio. Thanks also to Anne Williams, Anna Fox, Julian Rodriguez, and Helen Sear at the London College of Printing.

I would like to acknowledge Camerawork Gallery, London, who first showed *Homes and Gardens: Documenting the Invisible*, in 1996.

Special thanks to my amazing publisher, Frédérique Delacoste, for her belief in this book, for her unstinting support, and her adventurous spirit. Many thanks to my astute editor Felice Newman for her very fine work and to Don Weise for his support. Many thanks to designers Scott Idleman, Bernie Schimbke, and Ned Takahashi. Thanks to Karen Quigg for generous early support. Thanks to Simon Douglas at Metro Imaging, London, for printing the photographs.

I am very grateful to Marta Drury for the generous grant from the Heart and Hand Foundation, California, which funded my trips to Kosovo, and to Susan in the UK for her generosity. Thanks also to Judith and Duncan Peterson, Adrienne Hirt and Jeffrey Rodman, and anonymous sponsors. Many thanks to The John Kobal Foundation, London, for their grant, and to Metro Imaging, London for sponsorship.

Special thanks to my brother Nick and my parents Tony and Daphne for their love and support.

I only stayed four days on my first visit to Kosovo in the spring of 1989, but they were among the most intense four days of my life. Kosovo was an autonomous province within Serbia, with a population of 85 to 90 percent Albanians, until 1989, when Serbian President Slobodan Milošević planned to abolish Kosovo's special status and bring it under Serbian control. Mass protests began with the hunger strike of 1,350 Albanian miners at the Trepça (Trepča) mines and spread across the province, costing the lives of twenty-two protestors and two policemen. Still, Kosovo's autonomy was revoked.

I spoke with Kosova Albanian students in smoke-filled cafés where "the situation" was on everyone's lips. Foreign journalists were welcome, and my coffee was gratis. Unease and fear of the Serbian police were widespread. I found myself briefly under arrest and was searched by a Serbian policeman after photographing three women selling vegetables in the Prishtina (Priština) market. My Albanian companions wisely melted into the crowd. An Albanian policeman intervened on my behalf, joking with his Serbian colleague about giving me a hard time. On subsequent visits, I would meet only Serbian police—by the early 1990s, Albanian police had been replaced by Serbs—and

I rarely brought out my camera on the street.

I returned in 1992 to report for BBC radio and to write a diary of my experiences for *The Guardian*. I returned twice in 1993, and again in 1994 and 1995. My visits were short (no more than two weeks), partly because of visa restrictions and partly because of increasing surveillance and the risk of film confiscation or even of being thrown out of Kosovo, which had happened to several foreign photojournalists. The risk for local interpreters and drivers was much greater—of being detained in police stations, threatened, or beaten—but they were committed to informing the outside world. In 1994 and 1995, the roads were nearly deserted, save for a peppering of Serbian police checkpoints. One driver was Mehmet Aliu (interviewed in Chapter 7, "Past Present in Time Future"). Despite having been badly beaten up in a police station two months previously, Mehmet drove me to villages near Podujevë (Podujevo), not far from the border with "Serbia proper," and to remote villages near the Albanian border that had been raided by police.

Everyone had a story to tell, but it wasn't always easy to find publishable newspaper photographs. Repression was hidden, dramatic visual images rare. Police frequently cordoned off whole villages in the aftermath of police raids and beatings. How could you visually represent fear and repression in picturesque villages where roadblocks and surveillance of foreigners' movements made it impossible to witness such events?

I was shocked by the experience of sitting in sunny, immaculate living rooms listening to tales of extreme violence and terror. The summer visit in 1993, after two previous ones in the depths of winter, jolted me. One afternoon, I spoke with an old man who told me how he had been brutally beaten by police in his living room. We sat beneath a print of Constable's pastoral *Haywain* as he described how the police trampled over the flowerbeds as they pinned his son against the garden wall, threatening him with machine guns. When I returned the following year, the old man had died. I interviewed his son, Shyqri Ejupi, who tells the story of his father's beating (Chapter 1, page 12).

I wanted to try a different strategy from straightforward photojournalism. I began photographing the rooms and gardens where police raids had taken place. These images, accompanied by a soundtrack of Kosova Albanians speaking about their experiences, became an exhibition, *Homes and Gardens: Documenting the invisible*, a portion of which is reproduced here.

I photographed Serbian refugees who fled the Serb enclave of Krajina in Croatia in 1995 and had been resettled in Kosovo, living in appalling conditions in Prishtina. But the repression, beatings and torture experienced by Kosova Albanians remained the main focus of my work. While extensively documented by local and international human rights organizations, such as Amnesty International, the number of those killed remained comparatively small. The West was preoccupied with the Bosnian war and its atrocities, and Kosovo took a back seat.

The situation changed in the spring of 1998 when Kosova Liberation Army (KLA) actions against Serbian police led to large-scale reprisals and killings of civilians, particularly in Drenica. That summer, some 250,000 people, mostly Kosova Albanians, were reportedly displaced within Kosovo. Amnesty International estimated that more than 1,500 had been killed by the end of the year— many of the killings appeared to be extrajudicial executions. There were also reports of human rights abuses, including forcible displacements and abductions of people—listed as missing to this day—perpetrated by the KLA and other armed Kosova Albanians. The province was flooded with photojournalists and war correspondents.

In February 1999, I obtained a visa from the Yugoslav embassy with some difficulty and returned to see my Kosovar friends before the "spring offensive" feared by Balkan analysts. It was the time of the Rambouillet peace talks in France. Tension was high in Prishtina after a series of bomb attacks against Albanian-owned cafés and shops, but most people I met appeared hopeful that a settlement would be hammered out between the two sides. The Kosovo countryside however was anything but peaceful, as Shyqri Ejupi describes in Chapter 6, "Death Is Closer Than the Shirt You Are Wearing."

The following month, NATO bombs began to fall on Yugoslavia. My Kosova Albanian friends in London were desperate. In Prishtina, their parents (who were also my friends) awaited expulsion from their neighborhoods by Serbian police and paramilitaries. Every evening they sat in the dark, hoping that the paramilitaries would think the flat was unoccupied. They spoke on the phone in whispers. Then the phone lines went down. The London Kosovars endured many sleepless nights. We watched the war unfold on television, feeling angry, powerless, incredulous. My friends scrutinized every television news report for sightings of their parents. Would they make it across the border? At times, we feared their parents were dead. After ten days of silence, there was a phone call from Macedonia. They had survived.

I flew to Macedonia with a friend to see her parents who had found refuge with a family in Tetovo. While in Macedonia, I spent time with Miradije Aliu, whom I had met in 1994 when I was working on *Homes and Gardens*. Later, we spoke in the tent where she was living at Stenkovec 2, a refugee camp with a population of 22,000. I had an idea for a project. I knew I could not photograph nameless people crying as they streamed across the border on tractors, as in so many newspaper images I had seen. These pictures may have been necessary, but I could not bring myself to take them. I decided I would work slowly, taking studio style portraits of individuals, spending time with them over several visits, and listening to their stories—if they wished to tell them. I did not seek out sensational stories, the "worst" experiences. I looked for people I could engage with—a spark in the eyes, an intensity. This came first, then the talking, and finally the photograph. The time I spent in the camps in Macedonia was extraordinary, at times heart-wrenching, at times inspiring. People were very warm and hospitable, despite their difficult circumstances. I collected their home addresses in Kosovo—sometimes just the village name—and met everyone again on my return to Kosovo in the autumn of 1999 and in 2000.

The massacres in Kosovo committed by Serbian forces and paramilitaries dominated the consciousness of the Kosova Albanians I spent time with. In spring 2000, I photographed landscapes of massacre sites, accompanied by the survivors or the bereaved. Often there were only small clues to indicate a massacre had taken place; sometimes there were none. The stillness of these empty landscapes somehow echoed the empty rooms and gardens I had photographed in the mid-nineties. After two visits to Shefqet Avdia in Reçak (Račak), I found I was unable to sleep for many weeks. The urgent voice of this man describing the Reçak atrocity haunted my sleep. My friends, back in England, looking at a photograph of the Celinë (Celina) massacre site, would ask me, "What happened here?" And I just couldn't get the words out. If I felt like this, as a visiting photojournalist, what was it like for those who still lived in the same village where members of their families had been massacred? I was amazed by the resilience of the people I met.

That same spring, I visited Gračko, where fourteen Serb farmers had been shot dead in an apparent revenge attack. I followed a Swedish KFOR soldier for about a kilometer as he walked, head down, checking the ground for mines. The Kosovo Serbs strolled alongside us, careless of any danger, to the peaceful field where a Serb villager calmly recounted the horror of the massacre. I interviewed Kosovo Serbs, Roma, Ashkalia, Bosniaks, Turks, and Goranis. None of them, with the exception of Hashim Berisha, felt safe enough to have their portraits accompany their interviews; instead I photographed their living room, or KFOR sandbags banked outside their front door, or a landscape. Some Serbs were living in fear, surrounded by Albanian neighbors, with intermittent protection from KFOR, the NATO-led peacekeeping force in Kosovo; others lived in the comparative safety of enclaves. I would sometimes feel schizophrenic after spending the morning with a Kosovo Serb and the afternoon with a Kosova Albanian—listening to entirely differing versions of history.

Despite well-documented and well known eye-witness accounts of the massacres and extrajudicial executions by Serbian paramilitaries, police, and Yugoslav forces in Kosovo during 1998-1999 (estimates range from 6,000 to 10,000 Kosova Albanians killed; most sources quote the 10,000 figure), I still found people who denied these ever happened. Some Kosovo Serbs side-stepped questions by refusing to believe in what they had not personally witnessed. "I never saw anything," echoed the response of the Serbian official who had demanded years before, "Have you ever *seen* anyone beaten up on the street? No? Well then, how can you say it exists?" Meanwhile, Kosova Albanians were sometimes reluctant to concede that attacks on the Kosovo Serbs had been committed by their own people—except in self-defense. During my last visit to Kosovo, in February 2001, there was increasing tension and violence largely directed against Kosovo Serbs and Roma, who were perceived to be their allies. That same month, fighting between ethnic Albanian rebels and Macedonian forces began in Macedonia. The future for Kosovo remains uncertain and unpredictable.

A Note on Place Names

I decided to use *Kosovo* throughout rather than the spelling preferred by some, *Kosovo/a*, which is too awkward a construction to use frequently. Kosovo is neither the Albanian spelling *Kosova*, nor the full Serbian name *Kosovo Metohija*, but the internationally recognized name for the province, currently used by the United Nations.

When Albanians or Albanian-identified speakers are interviewed, Albanian spellings are used. When Serb or Slavonic language speakers are interviewed, Serbian place name spellings are used. When I am writing about Kosovo in my own voice, as in the case of chapter introductions, Albanian place names are used first, followed by the Serb name in parenthesis. In the taglines, the interviewee's preferred spelling appears first, followed by its alternative spelling in parenthesis. In the interests of brevity, Kosova Albanians, Kosovo Serbs, and Kosovo Turks are referred to simply as Albanians, Serbs, and Turks in the tagline and occasionally in the introductions. A glossary of place names appears at the end of the book. Nomenclature associated with Albanians use the Albanian form *Kosova* (e.g. *Kosova Liberation Army*).

Working with Interpreters

I speak some Albanian and understand a little Serbian, and often visited on my own when taking portraits, but I had to use interpreters for interviews. I worked with Kosova Albanian interpreters for Kosova Albanians, and Kosovo Serb interpreters for Kosovo Serbs, except for the interview with the Serb man I.S. in Prizren, when I was accompanied by a Bosniak (Muslim Slav) interpreter known to him. The Bosniak also interpreted for the Bosniak and Gorani interviewees. The interview with Hashim Berisha took place with an Albanian interpreter who worked at Plemetin (Plementina) camp. An Albanian woman from Prishtina interpreted for the interview with Shemsije (from the Roma community); they had met once before in a women's group. A United Nations High Commissioner for Refugees (UNHCR) officer interpreted for the interviews with the Kosovo Turks in Prizren. The security situation in Kosovo meant that it was not safe to travel with Serb interpreters outside their KFOR guarded apartment blocks in Prishtina without the security offered by an OSCE, UN, or KFOR vehicle. I relied on KFOR Serb interpreters for two of the interviews with Serbs. Several interviews were given in English—Edita Arifi in Neprošteno camp, Bujar Hoxha and Alban Ibrahimi in Čegrane camp, Dragana in Gorazhdec (Goraždevac), and Fatime Boshnjaku in Djakovë (Djakovica).

All interviewees were given the opportunity to remain anonymous, if they wished, as it was safer for them. Almost all the interviewees from the "minorities" chose to do so, as did two of the Kosova Albanians. Many of the transcribed interviews were checked with interviewees, either in person or by e-mail (which towards the end of my work, more and more Kosovars were able to access). Interviews were transcribed verbatim and carefully edited to maintain the sense of the whole. No effort has been made to correct obvious inaccuracies or add explanations—what is important is what the interviewees themselves believe.

The voices and images of the people of Kosovo will always stay with me—the urgency of Shefqet Avdia's voice as he described the Reçak massacre; the sight of Fahrije Gegollaj walking ahead of me up the path where "my son's bones have lain"; the intense conversations in Serb enclaves and Prizren cafés. I would like to thank all those who gave me their time, their trust, and relived their trauma to add their voices to this book.

Melanie Friend
London, May 2001

6

In 1994 and 1995, the majority of Kosova Albanians lived in a climate of fear under the harsh rule of Serbian president Slobodan Milošević. Albanian teachers and pupils had been excluded from the state secondary school system after a Serbian curriculum was imposed in 1991. The teachers organized illegal classes in Albanian in private homes, restaurants, garages, and half-built houses—one such schoolroom appears here. Pupils, teachers, and those who loaned their houses to the illegal schools ran the risk of harassment, arrest, and even brutal beatings. The Kosova Albanians organized peaceful resistance in the form of a parallel society, led by Dr. Ibrahim Rugova, head of the Democratic League of Kosova and unofficially elected President of the "Republic of Kosova" in 1992 by an overwhelming majority of Albanians. However, activists frustrated with the pacifist policies of Rugova began to organize an underground armed resistance, which later became the Kosova Liberation Army (KLA).

Out in the countryside, Serbian police conducted frequent and brutal raids on villages to search for guns. When journalists or other outsiders arrived, there rarely was any trace left of the violence. The police would cordon off the area for days or even weeks afterwards. By the time I was able to get to the village, the victims had fled or were in hiding, or the bruises were too faint to photograph. Besides, I could not—nor did I wish to—produce overdone shock-based photojournalistic images. Instead I was compelled to capture the tension between the beauty and quiet ordinariness of the homes and gardens I visited—where the violence had taken place—and the horror of the stories I heard directly from the Kosova Albanian residents.

HOMES AND GARDENS
DOCUMENTING THE INVISIBLE

1994-1995

No foreign journalists come here, so the police feel free to do what they want. In the small towns in Kosova, they do what they want.

They met me in the field outside the house. Right away, one of them grabbed me around the neck, and the other one kicked me, so I fell. About six or seven policemen kicked me continuously. They stopped when they thought it was enough and took me to the garden. There, another ten to fifteen of them beat me up. They hit me with anything they could. When they finished beating me, I was taken out by the wall. One of them pointed a machine gun at me while another took a packet of cigarettes from my pocket. A third got out some bullets and said that he would put them in my mouth instead of cigarettes…. When I got to the house, everything was broken, and my sixty-seven-year-old father was beaten almost to death. He was hit on the head with a truncheon and in the back with guns. My father died less than a year after this. He was very disturbed after what happened and never recovered.

We used to live in a village forty kilometers from here in the mountains where there were wolves and wild animals. So when the police came looking for arms, we gave them our two hunting guns. Here, in our house, nobody was beaten, but a woman was beaten a hundred meters from here—we saw her carried out on a stretcher. Maybe they didn't beat us because we gave up the guns, I don't know. We had eight police searching this room, but there was no maltreatment. Still, we are in a very dangerous situation. We are always frightened when we go outdoors.

Early one morning, at five minutes to six, someone knocked at my door, and we saw a policeman trying to get in. I told my husband to run away, opened the door, and about thirty policemen came into the yard. Five of them surrounded me. One of them hit me, while the others asked about my husband, ready to hit me with their machine guns. My children got frightened and went to another room; there were five in one bed and one in another. They were all sweaty from fear and didn't move at all for two hours. The police searched everywhere for my husband and then left. Immediately, I made the beds, thinking that they had really gone. I got my little two-year-old daughter, and was changing her nappies, when suddenly they came back. Three of them came into the house. They started searching all over again, and they were swearing and shouting at me....

My husband was in Austria visiting our son when the police came. There were about seventy of them, kicking the doors and chasing my mentally handicapped son. They asked, "Where is your husband?" My husband has a permit for a gun; I brought out the gun, and one policeman hit me hard in the face. I fell to the ground and was unconscious for three hours. Later, I was told that everyone had been screaming. My two boys were beaten in the yard and were left with bleeding hands. When my family said they must take me to hospital, the police said, "It's nothing if an Albanian dies." Now I have hypertension and high blood pressure, and at night I have nightmares of my sons being beaten. The police thought they'd killed me so they didn't stay more than an hour.

We have a lot of problems on our way to school. We are frightened of being stopped by the police, and anytime we see them we are afraid. But we carry on because we know that school is the most important thing. We have to study and not be assimilated.... Once when I was with a friend, we were stopped by police on our way home. They asked us for ID. My friend actually didn't have his ID on him; he had left it at home. They took him to the police station and beat him on the back of the head. The next thing he knew, he was in the hospital.

I hardly sleep at night, as I know that they may come at any moment…. Even that bit of sleep I get is a complete nightmare, full of frightening scenes with the police.

Sometimes I think I would rather die than live in this fear.

The police shouted, "Better surrender, otherwise we will roast you like a pig and use your skin to make wallets." My father shouted back, "Kosova Republic," "Never die Kosova," "Never die Albania".... Then the police began to beat up the children and to hold them in front of them, so my father couldn't fire. Only my father and I were left inside. My father said, "If the bullet hits me from the back, then you may cry for me because I'll have handed Kosova over to Serbia. If the bullet hits me from the front, then I don't want any of you to cry for me."

Suddenly, I saw him fall. He said, "My daughter, get out. The bullets got me." When the police found out that he was dead, they sang nationalistic Serbian songs and congratulated each other. The house was completely on fire. I managed to take him away from the fire just in time and kissed him on both cheeks in blessing. I covered his face with a handkerchief. Afterward, the police came and kicked his dead body. They said loudly to each other, "We'll kill all Albanians as we killed her father."

Then one of them took a butcher's knife and said, "Cut off his hand." I stretched out my hand, but he didn't do it. A second man pointed a pistol at my eye and threatened to kill me. This torture lasted from about 6:00 P.M. to 11:00 P.M. The next morning, I was taken to another room where they turned on the electric saw and threatened to cut off my head unless I told them about my friends and their activities…. I have lived in fear for the past year, and as I've got a wife and three children, I can't leave. So I stay at home, and every day I expect them to come back….

In the spring of 1999, about 850,000 Kosova Albanians (UNHCR estimate) were either brutally expelled from their homes or fled in fear of attack by Serbian paramilitaries and Yugoslav army forces. Approximately 445,000 fled to Albania, while 300,000 fled to Macedonia. The remainder fled to other countries in the region. In early April, tens of thousands of Kosova Albanians endured the horror of several days' wait in no man's land at Blace, as Macedonian authorities closed the border, fearful of an influx of refugees who would never leave. Some refugees died, trapped in the cold and rain. Once inside Macedonia, those with contacts or relatives lived with host families while the rest sought refuge in camps set up by UNHCR.

I visited Čegrane camp and was overwhelmed by its size (population exceeding 40,000). I decided to focus my work on a smaller camp, Neprošteno, which had a population of a mere 8,000. The camp was hot and dusty, but well organized with numbered rows of tents pitched very close together. Some families wrote their names and home village or town on the canvas. There was even a "main street," where the Albanians recreated the *korzo*, the evening stroll. This is where I first saw Vlora and Fatjon, whose portrait appears in this chapter, tiny figures marching confidently hand in hand down the main street. People seemed to enjoy the process of posing for studio style portraits, in front of a medium format camera on a tripod—perhaps it alleviated the boredom of camp life. Often a crowd of people looked on.

Initially, I worked with my friend Vlora, and later found interpreters within the camp: Diar Sinani (Mimoza's brother) and Edita Arifi, whose story appears here. I heard the words *Kurgjo, hiq* (*nothing, nothing*) frequently during my conversations in the camp. The refugees (or deportees) had taken nothing with them when they fled their homes, and they feared nothing would be left of their houses when they returned. These were not passive victims of historical events. Many had endured horrific experiences and had braved unimaginable journeys to reach safety.

During my return visit to Neprošteno in June 1999, the Yugoslav forces agreed to pull out of Kosovo. The Kosova Albanians began to anticipate their journey home.

All interviewees in this chapter are Kosova Albanians.

NOTHING, NOTHING

THE CAMPS:

MAY - JUNE 1999

We are from the village of Prugovc, near Prishtina. We were the last to leave our village because we were preparing the land for new crops. During our last month there, we were constantly harassed by the police. They robbed all the men in our family. My father-in-law had to plead with the Serbian police for the life of his son, my husband Avni.

Then Serbian police and paramilitaries burned our village. First they targeted families with sons in the KLA. I saw the Serbs burn one house at midnight, with the mother, father, and three children still inside. I saw a Serb neighbor burn down the house of an Albanian neighbor. The Serbs were working with the police, who gave them flame guns.

We fled at five in the morning. The police shot at us as we ran away in the dark. The Serbs had said, "You Albanians will pay for the NATO bombs." On one side of us, bullets were flying, and on the other side, our houses were burning. That night, NATO dropped a bomb on the petrol depot five kilometers away in Devet Jugoviq. We saw the blaze across the fields. On the way to the border, our tractors and our money were taken from us. I don't know how we managed to get here alive. We had nothing, no food, no water—only what we were wearing. At least we are alive. We survived.

Here in the camp, there's only bread and jam to eat, and we're scared our kids will get sick. We can't stay here. We have to get out of here.

Shqipe Pllana, age 24
Neprošteno camp, Macedonia, May 5, 1999

Shqipe and I live very close to each other, and we fled our homes together with our families. On our journey, we had to leave behind my aunt, her husband, and their family—their tractor broke down. We have no hope of seeing them again.

We've been in the camp for four days. We are four families in this tent—it's very crowded and dirty. There's nowhere to wash the kids. They cry all night long. They're so traumatized; Luarda has lost her appetite.

Luarda's a very spirited girl and spends most of her time with her aunts. She takes her personality from us, mostly from me. She's like a grown woman. She even walks like a woman. She has her own little bag of makeup, which she clung to when we fled our homes. Luarda loves being photographed and often pretends she's being photographed. She knows the words to one or two English pop songs, and every time she sees a model or a singer on TV, she says, "I want to be like her."

Lutfije Pllana, age 26, Shqipe's sister-in-law, and Luarda Pllana,
Shqipe's daughter, age 4
Neprošteno camp, Macedonia, May 5, 1999

The day after this interview, the Pllana family collected their copy of the daily newspaper Koha Ditore*, distributed free to refugees in the camp. Upon reading the paper, they discovered that seventeen of their relatives had been killed in Kosovo, including Lutfije's aunt's family whom they had had to leave behind. The names of their relatives were published in a list of the dead.*

The Serbian police harassed us before the NATO air strikes. When they came to our village again in early April, we hid in a neighbor's house and watched them loot our home. They tore up our documents and stole our gold. Then they shelled our village and we fled. We walked to the border, with police and paramilitaries constantly threatening to shoot us. Sometimes my brother carried my mother in a blanket; sometimes I supported her on one arm while I carried a twenty-kilogram bag with the other. I could hardly walk.

My brother is sick, and my father died nineteen years ago. I have to do both the women's work and the men's work of the family. My mother is my closest friend.

Myrvete Hyseni, age 35, right

My daughter Myrvete has always looked after me. On the journey here, she was crying all the time about me. I kept saying, "It's nothing, I'm all right," but she wouldn't stop crying. I had no food for four days and I thought I would die, but I worried so much about my children, it kept me alive.

The worst thing here is the heat and the children shouting. I have a constant headache. I just want to go back to Kosova and have the life I had before. I'm seventy-five years old and I miss my house. I miss all the things I worked for during those fifty-four years—the fields, the house, the land. I worry there is nothing left, that it's all gone. I used to grow tobacco in Kosova; I know how to make cigarettes and I like smoking. Here, I'm smoking more than usual, eight to ten a day.

Pashije Hyseni, age 75, left
Neprošteno camp, Macedonia, May 6, 1999 and June 16, 1999

I was a boy during World War I and was wounded while fighting in World War II. Then I was a soldier in Tito's time. Now I have three grandsons in the KLA.

Those last days in Vushtrri, we were living in fear. From our hiding place in the cellars, we saw people shooting, burning, and looting our house. They burned the mosque. Then we were ordered, "Just leave now!" We didn't even have a minute. Some of us ran away barefoot. Every morning, I ask my daughter-in-law to read me the newspaper to find out the names of those killed. All day, I think about Kosova, but I feel lucky I am still alive.

Behram Halili, Hanife, Astrit, and Shkelzen's grandfather, age 88

Neprošteno camp, Macedonia, May 11, 1999

I don't like anything about life in the camp. The Germans gave us some toys, but they don't change our life here. I paint pictures of my house and garden in Kosova all the time. I just want to go home, to a free Kosova. *Ishalla*, I believe I will.

Astrit Halili, Hanife's brother, age 11

Neprošteno camp, Macedonia, June 10, 1999

It's a nice life in the camp. We play, we walk around, we sit with our friends, we go to school. When my brother hurt his forehead, I went with him to the medical tent and watched everything the doctor was doing. Seeing the wounded and the sick in Kosova made me want to become a doctor. I'm an optimist. It's in my nature to be happy. Even at the moment we left our home, I always believed we would come back.

Hanife Halili, Astrit's sister, age 14
Neprošteno camp, Macedonia, June 14, 1999

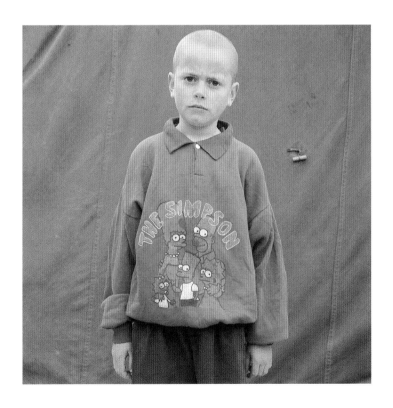

My dad sent me this sweatshirt. He left Kosova for Germany five years ago, when I was six. I think about him a lot. I don't know who the Simpson is. I'm making new friends in the camp, but I miss my friends in Vushtrri. The Serbs threw us out of our house. We had to move fast. I left my toys behind.

Shkelzen Halili, Hanife and Astrit's cousin, age 11
Neprošteno camp, Macedonia, June 10, 1999

Why did I buy this dress? Well, it was very hot, and I'd had several dresses like this which I'd had to leave behind in Kosova. So when I went to Tetovë on my visit out of the camp, I bought it. I wanted to make myself feel better.

I'm a classical singer, but I had to leave all my music behind. We had to leave the family violin, our books, all our family photos. I like choral music and sonatas—Bach, Schumann, Chopin, but Mozart's my favorite. I would like to sing in the camp, but there's no privacy.

Mimoza Sinani, age 20

Neprošteno camp, Macedonia, May 11, 1999

Mimoza Sinani's family fled their hometown of Gllogovc (Glogovac) on March 28 at 1:30 A.M. From their aunt's house, they watched Serbian police loot their home and burn it down. Surrounded by snipers and Yugoslav army forces, surviving on soup and macaroni, they finally were kicked out by police and arrived in Neprošteno on April 26.

We were on the move for a year before coming to Neproshten, living in the forests, constantly moving from village to village. From the hillside, we saw Serbian soldiers and police loot our home and burn it down. Everything was burned, gone, gone with the house. All we could save was ourselves. I don't care if I'm killed—all I care about is the safety of the children. I have five daughters, four sons, and ten grandchildren.

We finally arrived in Neproshten on May 8, after walking nonstop for twenty-three hours. We were warmly welcomed here and are grateful for the food, and now we have showers. But I'm old and can't stand the heat.

I kept my hat from Kosova, and I will never let anyone take it from me. The Serbian police used to say, "What do you need this hat for?" I didn't let them take it. It's our traditional Albanian hat and the Serbs don't like it. They would order me, "Take off your hat." They wanted to throw it in the fields. I was hit by the Serbian police four or five times because of my hat. They can kill me, but I won't take my hat off.

I sit all day and long for my village. All I want is to go back to Kosova. It's all I want. I want to be there.

Ramadan Avdia, age 73

Ne프rošteno camp, Macedonia, June 10, 1999

I come from Lipjan, a small town twenty kilometers from Prishtina. I used to travel daily to Prishtina to attend law school. The Serbian police often stopped me and my friends and sometimes confiscated our textbooks. They'd ask, "Why are you going to university? What's the point of studying? You'll be out of Kosovo soon." It made me even more determined to study.

After the bombing started, my family and I ran from the Serbian military and police for over a month. Then my father decided that my brother and I should leave for safety in Macedonia, while he and my mother would stay in Kosova. He said, "If you two are safe, then we will be OK." I didn't want to be separated from them, but I respected his decision. My mum packed two of my law books in my bag and said, "Wherever you are going to be, you should keep up your studies." She is a typist and wants more than anything in the world for me to become a lawyer.

The first day in the camp was terrible—I stayed inside the tent looking out at the people going past. I missed my mother and father. Now two months later, I still think about them all the time. I see them every night in my dreams: my mum says goodnight to me and hugs me.

I brought some family photographs with me, a little blue skirt my grandmother made for me when I was a year old with "Edita" embroidered on it in red, and the first shirt my eldest brother wore when he was born. My grandmother died last year. This is her last cigarette—she only smoked half of it, and I keep that with me. Every night I look at these things, and I feel my grandmother protecting me.

Edita Arifi, age 21
Neprošteno camp, Macedonia, June 13, 1999

In December 1998, my medical studies at Prishtina University were interrupted because of the conflict, so I signed up with the KLA. After serving six weeks, I took weekend leave and went home to Makovc to see Aurita, our three months old baby. That weekend fighting broke out nearby, and I couldn't go back to the army. My brother Driton and I patrolled the village as KLA observers; we also obtained medical supplies for our fighters. After an anti-aircraft vehicle came to Makovc, we left.

We hid in Prishtina for thirty-seven days. Both our Serb neighbors and local Roma in police uniform were looking for students (as many were in the KLA)—if they'd found us they would have killed us immediately. On at least twenty occasions, Driton and I had to hide in the sewers. We crouched on a narrow ledge for hours, right above the sewage, wearing medical masks to block out the terrible smell and the germs. The police walked right over the manhole, asking our parents, "Where are your boys?" Our parents kept saying we were abroad. Eventually, it became too dangerous and we fled to Macedonia, arriving at Neproshten camp on May 27.

It feels so incredible to be free, not to be frightened anymore, but I am sorry I'm here. I came here for my daughter's sake. I would have liked to stay and fight with my friends in Kosova.

Mentor Krasniqi, age 27
Neprošteno camp, Macedonia, June 16, 1999

After the bombing started, I was kicked out of my flat in Prishtina. I fled to Macedonia and started working with CARE, helping refugees at Çegranë. I worried about Alban, my best friend: What had happened to him? One day, I read in the Albanian newspaper that thirteen men had been shot dead by Serbian police in Alban's neighborhood. I kept asking about him.

On the morning of May 26, I came to work as usual to help a big crowd of new refugees. I suddenly saw this guy called Agim, who worked as a waiter with Alban, and there were Alban's father and mother. I was amazed. Then I saw Alban sleeping on a plastic sheet out in the open, under the sky. I woke him up. We were so happy! I hid from my boss and talked with him for hours. It was a very busy day for CARE. But my boss forgave me.

Bujar Hoxha, age 20, right

During the early days of the bombing in Prishtina, I would go out on the hill when it was safe and gaze at Bujar's block of flats in the distance. But it was too dangerous to go there.

On March 30, we were surrounded by snipers, and I saw a seventeen-year-old girl shot dead. We were thrown out of our homes, and for a week we found refuge in a ruined house. We ate flour contaminated with diesel. Then we fled to another village, but our host was shot dead. We came back to Prishtina. I saw the body of a man killed near my house. On May 24, my neighbors were beaten and their money stolen. The police told us, "Don't stay here, we can't protect you from our paramilitaries." At 4:00 A.M., we fled. In the train there were twenty-four of us in a small compartment. We slept standing up.

The next night, we arrived in Çegranë. I was so exhausted, I fell asleep under

the open sky. It was like sleeping on the best bed imaginable. When I woke up, I saw Bujar's face smiling above me, saying, "Hey, what are you doing here?" I hadn't seen any of my friends for a long time. I was so surprised, and so happy. I cannot express what I felt in words…

Alban Ibrahimi, age 20, left
Čegrane camp, Macedonia, June 12, 1999

The walk to the border took eight hours, but Vlora managed to walk by herself most of the way. It was cold and raining. The kids were crying. To keep them going, I told them, "We're going to visit your father in Germany." Now in the camp, she keeps asking me, "When are we going to see our father? You promised me…" A month ago, she met Fatjon; they're inseparable. I let them go on short walks around the camp on their own. We can trust people to look after them.

Jalldëze Rexhepi, mother of Vlora, age 3

On the train to the border, Fatjon stayed close to his uncle, he loves him so much. There were two policemen near us. One ordered us into a compartment and threatened to shoot us, but when the other saw Fatjon, he said, "He's so beautiful," and gave him some chocolate. Fatjon wanted to eat the chocolate but his uncle didn't let him—he was worried that the chocolate was poisoned. Then the policeman got angry, so Fatjon ate the chocolate.

On the train, Fatjon sang KLA songs. We said, "Fatjon, don't mention the KLA because the police are right near us!" but he didn't listen. Sometimes he sings and pretends he has a gun. When he sees the Macedonian police here in the camp, he shouts "UÇK!" *

He is so close to Vlora, he tells everyone she is his sister. They wash and dress Vlora's doll, and spend all day, every day, together.

Bahti Gashi, father of Fatjon, age 3
Neprošteno camp, Macedonia, June 15, 1999

* Ushtria Çllrimtare e Kosovës (Kosova Liberation Army)

When the air strikes started, we hid in the bunker because we were afraid of the paramilitaries. My husband Mehmet had built this bunker at the end of the garden all by himself in anticipation of war fifteen years ago. The ceiling was three meters high and there were three exits: it had a toilet, two air conditioners and electricity. It was covered with grass. About three hundred of us, women and children, hid down there every night for ten nights. The men were on guard all night. There was only room to sit; it was impossible to sleep. We could hardly breathe. We were scared of being poisoned by chemicals. We were terrified of being raped or killed.

On March 29, there was a battle at our house. Three neighbors were killed. The Serbs destroyed the house we had loaned to the school and Mehmet's brother's house. But they didn't find the bunker. When the KLA soldiers came to rescue us, we ran for our lives, avoiding Arkan's men in the streets. I only had the clothes on my back and the slippers on my feet. I hid my earrings under my scarf so the Serbs wouldn't pull them from my ears.

At Bllace we were left without food for four days and four nights in the mud and rain—we had nothing, nothing. On the fifth day, I lost consciousness and was carried to a Red Cross hospital.

It's so hot here in Stankovec. There are no showers, and the toilets are filthy. I always feel dirty. I'm in a foreign country and I feel helpless and demoralized. I wouldn't wish this even on my enemy.

I did not have time to say goodbye to Mehmet—he just told me to run away as fast as I could. My heart is so dark now. I have had no news of him since we fled. I don't know if I will ever see him again.

Miradije Aliu, age 51
Stenkovec 2 camp, Macedonia, June 3, 1999

On April 1, masked paramilitaries came to our house in Prishtina and threw us out. Luckily, we were prepared because the adjoining neighborhood had already been cleared. We had some clothes and two kilos of bread packed and ready. We had buried jewelry in the flowerbeds.

We were stuck at the border for seven days. We slept in the car. We were so scared that our daughter, Sanija, would be taken. We finally arrived safely in Neproshten on April 8.

It's been a shock adjusting to the conditions in the camp, but we feel lucky to be alive. I'm a homemaker; I tried to make the tent into our home but it's impossible. I cook and clean all day, wash clothes as often as possible—it keeps me calm.

Before we fled Kosova, our son Arben, who's fifteen, was so scared of the Serbs he had to take tranquilizers. He doesn't want to go back to Kosova because he's afraid the paramilitaries and police are still there. We think he'll get over it as soon as he sees the NATO soldiers.

Tomorrow we return home, and I'm very happy. We'll leave at 3:00 A.M. to avoid the traffic and the crowds. I hope to find our home the way we left it. The Serbs are robbing on their way out of Kosova, so we must get back quickly. The only thing that scares me are the mines.

Sofia, age 47

Neprošteno camp, Macedonia, June 17, 1999

The massacre of Kosova Albanian civilians at Reçak (Račak) on January 15, 1999 was a pivotal event in the Kosovo conflict. This event hardened American and European resolve to back up diplomatic efforts with the threat of military intervention against Yugoslavia. The day after the massacre, OSCE Kosovo Verification Mission observers visited the site thirty kilometers from Prishtina (Priština). Ambassador William Walker, head of the OSCE Mission, immediately accused the Yugoslav authorities of responsibility for the massacre. The Serbian government claimed that the dead were combatants and that Reçak had been stage-managed to look like a massacre for propaganda purposes. The international human rights organization Human Rights Watch and a Finnish forensic team confirmed that the forty-five bodies found at Reçak were those of unarmed civilians. On May 27, 1999, Slobodan Milošević was indicted for war crimes in Kosovo by the International Criminal Tribunal for the former Yugoslavia in The Hague (ICTY). The massacre at Reçak was cited specifically. The killings at Lubizhde (Ljubižda) and Celinë (Celina) have also been documented by international human rights organizations.

Survivors of massacres, or relatives of those killed, often take on the role of escorting visitors to the graveyard or to the massacre site. They become guides for human rights workers, journalists, foreign and local visitors. Often bereaved and traumatized themselves, these men and women are the safekeepers of memory, historians for their communities. Shefqet Avdia, a villager from Reçak, told me I was the first foreign journalist to have heard his story; I was the twenty-second foreign journalist to have heard Qerim Nerjovaj's story of the massacre at Lubizhde in the Has region.

The following accounts describe three of the massacres of Kosova Albanians committed by Serbian paramilitaries, police and Yugoslav Army soldiers during 1999.

The interviews at Reçak and Lubizhde were recorded on site; the following accounts are edited transcripts. All interviewees in this chapter are Kosova Albanians.

THE GUIDES

Reçak (Račak)

On April 27, 2000, I followed Shefqet Avdia, a forty-eight-year-old Reçak villager up a rocky path to the top of a hill, the site of a massacre that took place on January 15, 1999. We were accompanied by interpreter Edita Arifi.

Shefqet Avdia: …They were shooting with the tanks. The Serbian soldiers were walking between the houses, trying to capture the people, and then the women and children and everyone started running away and did their best to hide somewhere… *(noise of low-flying plane overhead)*

Edita Arifi: *(breathing heavily)* Oh, my god, can you imagine they escaped here, up this hill? it's very hard to walk here…. This is the place, is it?

Shefqet Avdia: …so the people came here. Policemen—Serbs—were hiding here, expecting them. I heard the Serbs saying, "Anyone under fifteen years old, don't touch, but upwards of sixteen or seventeen years old, just kill them…." The people, when they were captured here, were made to stay in line, and every one of them was shot, and after that with a…very nice knife…they took eyes from the faces and hearts from the chests, and the Serbs later said, "That's not true, we didn't do that," the mice, they'd eaten them… *(pointing to the ground)* The people were captured exactly in this spot and they were shot—see the marks? There's a red stone, there was a man killed here, and then a blue mark there, there was a man killed there also, and you have marks all the way up there. *(footsteps over stones, walking up the hill)* See this one, too? It's a red cross. From down there to up here, the men, the people were killed, lots of marks, see here…

Melanie Friend: Did you come up to see the bodies afterwards?

Shefqet Avdia: *(emphatically)* My friends and I couldn't go outside. Serbian police were shooting until four or five in the afternoon. When the observers arrived in the morning, we went with them to see the place where the people were murdered. Three of us stayed here all night to guard the bodies. *(softly)* One of the victims was my cousin. He wasn't dead, but he was fighting not to let his soul go out of his body, so he crawled up here. This is how he was found dead after all, and the

Serbs who found him took his heart and things from his body and put them on the top of his stomach. *(silence for few seconds, then sound of footsteps through bushes, undergrowth)* You can see this is where they cut his neck. They took out his eyes and the things from his chest. *(silence)*

That night, I was at my neighbor's, eating whatever we had to eat. We thought we would soon be dead, like our friends, that there were no days left for us. I felt very, very sorry about the people who were killed. I thought that I would never be able to live after that.

For three months, I was very, very sick and couldn't even go to the toilet by myself. I thought I'd never be able to walk again. I was in big trouble. Thirteen members of my family were killed here. I kept thinking over and over, "Why wasn't I in that group? Why wasn't I shot?" But it wasn't my destiny to die. (*silence*)

I recovered slowly, with injections and some strong tranquilizers my friends brought from Switzerland. I still have the tablets. I still use them. Sometimes I sleep well. Sometimes I stay awake all night, talking with the souls of my friends who were killed here. When I talk to them, it's like they are all alive. *(wind, birds chirping, a tractor in distance)*

I believe that until I am dead, I will not forget. This memory will never come out of my brain. (*silence*)

Lubizhde (Ljubižda)

On October 21, 2000, Fahrije Gegollaj, age forty-nine (seen in photograph), and Qerim Nerjovaj, age twenty-five, and I walked up a steep hill to the site of a massacre that took place on April 12, 1999. We were accompanied by interpreter Rresearta Reka.

Fahrije Gegollaj: I've only been up here four or five times. Six months after the massacre of our men, their fathers and brothers went up the mountain to pick up the bones. The internationals helped them. I came out of my house to see whatever was left of my son—but there was nothing to be seen but bags…. We buried his bones in the village. My son Nexhat was only twenty-two years old…he was our son, a son, and we will never see him again…. Let's go, we have to go up there…it's pretty far, up by those tall trees.

Thank you for coming to see where my son's bones have lain…. This is our sons' road, our sons have fallen on this path, so this is our sons' path…

Rresearta Reka: Coming up here makes me think I never want to live with the Serbs again, and if they come back, I'm going to Australia or New Zealand, as far away as I can get. This path is so difficult…. They could have just shot them where they were back there and not make them suffer and flee up these hills.

Fahrije Gegollaj: *(pointing to the ground)* This is my husband Haxhi's jacket…. He was wounded here. The first time they lined him up for an execution, he didn't get shot, but the second time, he was wounded…. When they shot our son dead, my husband couldn't even turn around to look because his hands were tied behind his head…. (*walking over rocks and dead leaves, low voices*)… This is where it happened.

Qerim Nerjovaj: Many families gathered on this hillside for safety, but on April 12 at 7:30 in the morning, the Serbian soldiers and paramilitaries caught up with us, separated us from the women and children, and made us men sit here. Then they divided us into groups of eight and asked each group, "Who wants to die first? Which ones of you want to see your friends die?" They took eight of us and lined us up for execution. The first bullet hit my left leg, the second shot I got on my fore-

head, right here. We all fell neatly in a line. After I fell to the ground, I got another bullet in the hand when a soldier shot a last round into us. I was wounded but still conscious, lying in the water. I could hear the soldiers eating and drinking. Then they forced the surviving men to get our bodies and spread them around because they feared NATO might take aerial photographs. If they spread the bodies around, then NATO would think we were KLA soldiers killed in battle.

Her husband was only wounded, and as he stood up, the Serbs said, "Oh, you're still alive," and then his son said, "Oh, dad, you're still alive," and the Serbs said, "Now you will see what we are going to do to your son," and they shot a whole magazine into his son's body.

Fahrije Gegollaj: They sent the women and the children down the mountain. In the spring, there is a river here, and while they were going down, they could see the blood flowing past them.

Qerim Nerjovaj: Her husband was spared because they had killed his son, so they didn't need to kill him as well. Then they took all the men who were left, tied them up, and sent them down the hill. When the soldiers had gone, I managed to get up and check if any other men had survived, but none of them moved. I stayed up here for four days until it was safe to go home.

Fahrije Gegollaj: Two weeks after the massacre, my husband joined us in Albania and told us what had happened. I couldn't cry as much as I wanted, because I wasn't in my own country. If we'd been at home, we could have banged our heads against the wall or done whatever we wanted. It's still inside me. I didn't manage to let it all out. My cousin's son was one of those forced to spread the bodies around, and when he joined us in Albania, he couldn't do anything for a week, he couldn't even sleep. His nerves were shattered. He stared down at the floor all the time. He wouldn't speak. *(silence, then footsteps)*

Qerim Nerjovaj: This is the twenty-second time I've been here with a foreign journalist. When I come here with others, I try to be as strong as I can. When I come alone, I cry a lot, and it seems that my friends are all alive again…. I take tranquilizers every night—no way can I sleep without them. Everywhere I go, there are traces of what happened. Every time I come here, I notice different bits of clothing, and then in the night I see them in my sleep. When I come to this place, I think of what happened here, and when I go to see my burned house, I remember it was burned by the same people…. On the road to Prizren, I remember being beaten at the crossroads by the Serbian police. When I go to market, I remember when police forced me off the bus. When I'm alone, I get flashbacks. I'm only twenty-five, but because of the things I've seen, I feel very old—I have seen what one human being can do to another.

Fahrije Gegollaj: We mothers who have lost our sons go to our daughters' homes to relax—we cannot relax anywhere here in the village. If we sit at home, we just think about it more….

Rresearta Reka: I don't know how they cope with it. Every morning they wake up and look out of the window—the first thing they see is that hill over there where the killings happened. It's so beautiful here, but what a terrible history.

Celinë (Celina)

On April 22, 2000, I went to Celinë with interpreter Edita Arifi to find the place where villagers had been killed on March 25, 1999, the day following NATO's first air strikes. When we arrived, a young man, Hajdar Zeqiri, offered to take us there. After walking for about four hundred meters, he stopped by the edge of a ploughed field, pointed a few meters to our right, and said:

This is the spot where my four sisters, my brother, my mother, my cousin and his wife, my other cousin's bride, and my cousins' children were killed by Serbian paramilitaries…. Altogether nine children and four adults died here.

The vast majority of Kosova Albanian refugees returned soon after NATO forces entered Kosovo on June 12, 1999.

I have seen all those whom I met in the camps again, back in Kosovo, but it has not always been easy to find them. The postal system was not functioning, and telephones in the villages were rare. On the smaller roads, signposts were nonexistent. Sometimes I would travel all day with the hope that the person I wanted to see would happen to be at home.

In September 1999, as I tried to find Ramadan Avdia, villagers en route told my interpreter that nobody was left in his village, Koshtanjevë (Koshtandjeva). Luckily, on a remote, very narrow road, we crossed paths with a Polish KFOR jeep. The soldiers offered to take us to Koshtanjevë in their jeep, bumping and swerving up one of the worst mountain roads in Kosovo. At the top of the track, we met a young girl with Ramadan Avdia's eyes; she was his granddaughter, and she led us to him. When I returned in October 2000, I was not so lucky; the KFOR vehicle I was traveling in went off the road into a deep ditch. When I walked up the rest of the hill to find Ramadan Avdia, I found that he had chosen that very day to make his annual visit to his daughter, walking for three hours across the mountains to her village.

I also met Remzie Neziri, whom I had interviewed in 1995 (Chapter 1, page 15).

There were many shared experiences among these returnees—the discovery that relatives had been killed, that homes had been burnt or looted, or for some, the relief of finding their homes had been untouched. Some of those I met suffered post-war traumatic stress. They had felt better back in the camps. Help from the internationals was felt to be inadequate and slow. There was energetic reconstruction in much of the province; grocery stores and internet cafés sprung up in the Prishtina neighborhood where I was staying. But for the majority, there was no way of earning a living. Interpreters and drivers working for the internationals were among the fortunate minority, earning at least DM1000 per month, five or six times the average income in Kosovo. Few factories were operating, and salaries for teachers, academics, and public employees were extremely low. Many relied on humanitarian aid.

All the Kosova Albanians I met felt relieved to be free after ten years of repression. They were grateful to the KLA and to NATO for its intervention and its continuing presence. But after the initial euphoria, some of the old fears returned. In post-war Kosovo life is not safe—organized crime is rife. Raids by masked, armed men are common.

"Mud is sweeter in your homeland than honey anywhere else" is a translation of an old Albanian saying, "Në vendin tënd është më e ëmbël balta se ne vend të huaj mjalta."

MUD IS SWEETER IN YOUR HOMELAND THAN HONEY ANYWHERE ELSE:
THE RETURN

On June 14, two days after NATO arrived, we made our way back to Kosova. I was very frightened, even though we were in a convoy escorted by KFOR. I felt like it was doomsday. We saw a desert, a dead place, not a living soul anywhere, and lots of houses burning. Everything was in ruins. Prishtina was paralyzed—rubbish was everywhere, no shops were open. KFOR was everywhere on the streets.

We'd last seen our home in the middle of the night on March 29, when we fled terrified from the bunker. That night I thought I will never be able to come home again, I will never see my husband again, no one will survive this war. On June 14 we were back, and as we came through the front gate, everything smelled of ash and human shit.

We saw the house we had loaned to the school all charred and burnt, but fortunately, the walls of our little house were still standing. There was glass all over the floor, and the cupboards were broken. The Serbs had stolen our cutlery and crockery, even the teaspoons. They'd used knives on the furniture, shat and peed on our family photos and on our clothes. The Serbian police and paramilitaries had slept in our cousin's house, but they deliberately had used our home as a toilet. They'd scrawled Serbian crosses, crude sexual drawings, and graffiti on the walls: "Serbia to Tokyo," "We will rape you," "If you come back here we will eat you," "We will massacre you." I felt like dying. It's unbelievable what human beings can do....

It took us women—eight of us—six weeks to clean the house. All our men were still in the KLA. In the beginning, we had nowhere to sleep; we sat outside on the sofas all night or lay on the blankets we'd brought from Macedonia. We were very tired and still frightened. We had no Serbs in the neighborhood before, only Gypsies, but we were never friendly with them. During the war, our cousins saw Gypsies come into this house. The Gypsies fled because they did what the Serbs did.

As for the Serbs, I have no sympathy for them at all—none of them are innocent. The Serbs killed our children. I don't believe that they are having a bad time or that they can't go out to buy food. I think it's a lie. A few weeks ago, the Serbs threw grenades in Lipjan. If any Serbs were killed, then maybe the KLA killed them in self-defense while they were trying to bring

peace to this country. I won't feel safe until there are no more Serbs here in Kosova.... No human race has suffered as much as the Albanians.

Several in my family have been killed, although my husband and my kids all survived. In February 1999, in Prishtina, my eighteen-year-old girl cousin went to buy sugar and was killed in a bomb attack in the shop. Then Serbs killed my twenty-two-year-old cousin while the fighting was happening around our houses—he was shot near our neighborhood while trying to escape. My husband's nephew was killed after the war while out working with KFOR—he took a lunch break under a tree with his cousin and the road collapsed underneath them. He was suffocated. Another cousin of my husband, twenty-seven years old, was in a bus that was mistakenly bombed by NATO. That was the bus on the bridge at Lluzhan.

I still feel pleasure being back home and walking around town. It's so good not seeing the police everywhere—only NATO soldiers waving at us. Before the war, I was constantly looking out of the window, terrified that the police would come and kill my husband and my family because of the school. Now it is time to work and rebuild, *Ishalla*. We'll live like independent people in a free Kosova and the Serbs will not rule us.

Miradije Aliu, age 51
Prishtina (Priština), September 30, 1999

When I was in the camp, I heard that Koshtanjevë, my village, had been completely burned down. We left the camp on June 23, and on the journey back to Kosova, we were told by locals along the route that not a living soul was left.

When we arrived, we found our house still standing—but nothing else. The Serbs had taken our TV and our fridge, everything. They had left the door of the house open and there was cow shit everywhere. It took a month before the house was livable. We'd brought groundsheets with us from the camp and we slept in the open. We ate nothing but cherries for the first week. We used to have forty hens and two cows, but the Serbs must have taken them. Now we get a little aid—flour, oil, rice, beans, a little canned beef—but in the last two months only the Polish KFOR soldiers have come to see how we are.

We used to pass the time of day with our Serb neighbors—"How are you? How are you surviving?"—until the Serbian police started hassling us. And since they routed us out, we're not talking to them anymore. It's great not having the police around now, but still we don't feel free. Our village is surrounded by Serb villages, and we're scared that the Serb villagers will come here and kill us. We've got nothing to defend ourselves with and would have to flee to the forest—but we believe that somehow KFOR would save us.

We're very cut off here; our village is inaccessible by car, we've never had a telephone, and now we have no TV or radio. We don't have any money. I have only the clothes I am wearing, and I'm worried about the winter.

Ramadan Avdia, age 73
Koshtanjevë (Koshtandjeva), September 25, 1999

My parents returned home to Lipjan before me. VJ soldiers had been living in our flat during the last weeks of the war. There was graffiti in the toilet and human shit everywhere; our clothes were all over the place. They found needles, alcohol, and spoons for cooking heroin.

Our Montenegrin neighbor, who married a Serb, noticed how the Serbian paramilitaries and the Roma were stealing TVs in Lipjan and took our TV, video, and tape recorder to her flat for safety. The paramilitaries would have been angry had they known. She was a very decent neighbor. My mum and she would walk in and out of each other's flats without knocking and would fight good naturedly about politics, Serbs and Albanians, and end up laughing. Two or three months after NATO arrived, she left Kosova. She couldn't live with the fear. When I saw her fear, I remembered how my mother and I had lived in terror of Serbian reprisals when NATO started bombing in spring 1999.

The day I started work as an interpreter at the British base in Lipjan, I saw all the guys talking together in English, and I thought I was in a movie. It was the most exciting job I'd ever had. I was proud to work with the British soldiers and felt powerful in my uniform, although I was a little embarrassed because I was in my home town and everyone stared at me. The British soldiers knew how to enjoy life—"Life is short," they'd say—but they swore every second and tried to make me swear. They were too open and too free in the way they talked.

I didn't mind translating from Serbian with the old people, knowing it would help KFOR. Some of them knew a little Albanian, and to make my job easier sometimes, they'd slip into Albanian. I met one old Serb woman who was happily surprised that I was doing this work. I behaved the same towards the Serbs as towards the Albanians.

Edita Arifi, age 22
Lipjan (Lipljan), October 4, 1999 and November 1, 2000

It's good to be home. Now we can go anywhere freely, and we like the NATO soldiers very much. But my good friend Muhamet's father and his two brothers were killed in spring 1999.

Our school was damaged, and for the first two months we had lessons outside. In our history class, we are studying the Illyrians, and how they used to fight, and how Skënderbeg prevented the Ottomans from ruling what was then Albania. We are also studying King Stefan of the Serbs who occupied some Albanian regions. Our teacher says that our relationship with Serbs was already bad then. We are learning about the

Serbs occupying seven hundred Albanian villages and deporting the Albanian villagers. I've always liked history. Since the war, it's become more interesting to me than art. I want to know more about how Albanians used to live in the past. I am learning that Albanians have always suffered and that the Turks, like the Serbs, oppressed the Albanian nation.

The teacher never says the Serbs are our enemies, but everyone knows they are. I know both from books and my own experience how the Serbs occupied us and forced us to go to Macedonia. I haven't seen any Serbs since I came back, except one day when Muhamet and I went to fetch firewood nearby, we saw old Serbs working in the fields. I wouldn't have a Serb friend, I never had one, never will. I don't need any. I have enough Albanian friends.

Astrit Halili, age 13
Vushtrri (Vučitrn), October 14, 2000

I n previous wars, they never destroyed the mosques and churches—only in this war. I feel sorry for the Serbs whose churches have been destroyed, because the Serbs also pray, in their own language. I am for those who are religious, who believe in God. The man without faith, he will kill children.

Behram Halili, age 89

Vushtrri (Vučitrn), April 28, 2000

Behram Halili died on February 11, 2001.

My husband used to be a poorly paid city bus driver. Now he works as an electrician for the U.S. office and is on a very high salary. When we first returned to our house after the war, he would come home so tired from his work, he just went to sleep. I was home all day doing house-work. I kept reliving our flight from Prishtina to the refugee camp. When I saw my women friends, it's all we talked about. I had high blood pressure and dizzy spells and found it difficult to sleep.

Then, Arben, my son, was run over by a car last February, and I was so anxious about his health that I began to forget about the war. I remember him lying in bed in hospital, writhing in pain while unconscious. He's better now, but I can't stop thinking of the moment when he was hit by the car and I didn't know if he would live or die.

Now that we have more money, we can finish building our new house. As for our Serb neigh-bors, they left after the NATO bombings, and I'm happy never to see them again. When I see TV reports on Serb enclaves, I remember the day they threw us out of our house, and I think, "Why is KFOR protecting them?" The Serbs killed a lot of people. They do not deserve to be protected. I am not angry with KFOR for protecting innocent, ordinary people—but those who committed atrocities…. I cannot blame old people and Serb housewives, but I blame the para-militaries and the police. I could imagine living in the same city as innocent Serbs—if others didn't object. I would not be comfortable with them as neighbors, but if they lived on the other side of the city, I could tolerate it. But the trust is lost.

Sofia, age 48
Prishtina (Priština), October 27, 2000

We came back to Makovc on June 30, 1999. We found a desert, a dead village. There was garbage everywhere. There was no work and no money, and so I decided to give up my medical studies and registered with UNMIK to become part of the civilian police force. I was excited by the idea of joining the Kosovo Police Service and working with the internationals. I wanted to catch drug dealers, that kind of thing.

I was called for training in July 2000. We were about three hundred Albanians, twenty Serbs, and some Turks and Bosniaks. We attended class together for two months but kept separate during the breaks. The trainers were all English and there were two translators, one interpreting for the Albanians, one for the Serbs. I focused on my training and never spoke to the Serbs.

I work at the police station in the center of town. There are no Serb police here, and none in Prishtina either, as far as I know. In the Prishtina region, there are Serb policemen in Graçanicë. I think in Obiliq and Fushë Kosovë, there is a mixed police force. We only earn DM 350 per month as trainees, but we all work very hard. The biggest problem we come up against in our station is car theft.

I am busy with my work—I hardly think about the war anymore. But my wife still takes tranquilizers and goes for therapy with an Albanian neuropsychiatrist. After we came back in summer 1999, she had nightmares—visions of dead bodies, and Serbian police chasing her. She watched TV nonstop and talked with her friends all the time about the war and took it all to heart.

Mentor Krasniqi, age 28
Makovc (Makovce), February 15, 2000 and February 13, 2001

We had had Serbian officers sleeping in our house. They used it as their local head-quarters. When we came back, we found their graffiti on the walls: "Fuck your Albanian mother," "Albright, you old bitch, do you want an Albanian dick?" "Tony Blair, you're not fair," "We will be back," "This is Serbia."

I didn't want to come back to Kosova. I couldn't imagine life without my brother Avni, my sister-in-law Shqipe, my nieces Luarda and Aurela. Luarda was like my own child—when she cried, she called my name. I never expected us to be separated. When I said goodbye to her in Stankovec, she didn't cry. She just waved very slowly. It was the worst moment of my life. I could never love anyone more than Luarda.

At first, Luarda would speak to me on the telephone from England. But one day, I rang her and said, "Luarda is that you? It's Lutfije," and she said, "Oh, OK," and passed me on to her mum. I was so upset I hung up. Now she loves going to school in Southport and has learned a lot of English. She rarely asks about me—when I sent photos to Shqipe and Avni in England, Luarda didn't even look at the picture of me. The love might come back, but I'm not sure.

A month ago, Avni and Shqipe made Luarda speak to me on the phone. She asked, "Are the police still there? Are the Serbs still there? Did they take away my dolls?" She is still frightened of the police—because of the trauma of seeing them nearly kill her dad. I cannot forget that day either.

Every day, I spend about DM 30 speaking to my brother on my mobile phone. My dad says, "We must take it away from you!" All my wages go to pay the phone bill; I never save any money. I can't help it.

Lutfije Pllana, age 27

Prishtina (Priština), October 5, 1999 and October 17, 2000

Lutfije's brother Avni, sister-in-law Shqipe, and her nieces Luarda and Aurela moved from Neprošteno to Stenkovec camp in May 1999. From there, they were flown to England with the UNHCR Humanitarian Evacuation Programme. Lutfije moved back to Kosovo in late June 1999.

Our first night in England, we felt so sad and far from home. My parents were still in Kosova, and we didn't know if they were alive or not. The Serbs would have burned my entire village, Sekiraçë, if KFOR hadn't arrived. They killed my brother when he went back to see what had happened to his burnt house. My uncle and aunt were killed with their four children. My husband Avni lost seventeen relatives.

Two days after NATO's air strikes began, Serbian police came to my aunt's house in Prishtina, where we had taken refuge. They arrived early one morning while Avni was playing with Luarda, and accused him of being in the KLA. They threw bullets on the kitchen floor and said to him, "These are for you." They took him out into the garden. Luarda was screaming, "Daddy, the police are going to kill you!" I can never forget her screaming through the closed window, "Dad, come back!" I was frantically looking for my gold jewelry to give to the police to save Avni's life. From the garden, the police saw Luarda crying at the window—maybe she and God helped him survive. The police decided to ring the police station, who confirmed that Avni had a clean record. They released him.

Our first four nights in England, Luarda woke up screaming, "The police are here…Where's daddy?" On the fifth night, a social worker at the reception center asked Avni what was happening. The social worker suspected him of abusing our daughter. When we explained, he said he felt sad and ashamed that he hadn't realized Luarda would have nightmares because of what had happened in Kosova. She had nightmares every night for our first two weeks in England, but we didn't go to a psychologist because we know she's very scared of doctors: she thinks they are some kind of police.

Last weekend, there was an air show in Southport. Luarda was terrified. She pointed up at the planes and cried out "NATO! UÇK!" We had to explain to the local people that we were from Kosova. We like Southport a lot. It's very quiet and safe. We were always scared of everything in Kosova, the water, the biscuits, always checking the food in case the Serbs poisoned it.

The very first time I saw police here, I was scared, but their uniform is so different from the Serbian police, and we hardly ever see them. One day, Luarda saw a police car with its blue

lights flashing. She dropped her ice cream, ran to Avni, and wrapped her arms round his legs screaming "Milicia! Police!" Avni said, "Don't worry, these police don't want to kill me."

I miss Kosova a lot and the people I lost. I just ache for the people. It doesn't matter that we lost our house—with God's help we will rebuild. But to be in Kosova, and feel the absence of people…My father says that in Kosova, everywhere you turn, people cry and feel miserable.

Shqipe Pllana, age 25, and Luarda Pllana, age 4
Southport, England, September 7, 1999

When we came back from Albania and saw the walls of our house still standing, we felt so happy. The washing machine, TV, satellite dish, deep freeze, electricity generator, and our tools had all gone, but we didn't care.

In 1995, our son Bashkim was beaten up by the police and began to have epileptic fits. In February, 1999, after the Reçak massacre, he left for Austria. He was terrified, couldn't sleep all night, and kept saying, "Here they come, they are coming now to massacre us!" Now he's back with us, but still has the same nightmares. He's seen a neuropsychiatrist and is still on tranquilizers.

I have bad dreams too—and my back has been hurting me ever since that day in 1995 when the police hit me. I will always remember that day, even more than the day we fled to Albania. It was the worst day of my life. If I don't take tranquilizers, I don't sleep at all. I wake up screaming, imagining the police are coming. We live near Mitrovicë, and we are fearful of what might happen there.

Remzie Neziri, age 51
Ugmir (Dobra Luka), September 26, 1999 and October 14, 2000

Mitrovicë (Kosovska Mitrovica) on the opposite page, is a divided city, with a bridge over the river Ibar separating the northern Serbian part of town from the southern Albanian side. Attempts by Albanians to return to their homes and jobs in the north under KFOR protection have led to violent clashes. Frustration with the lack of progress has led to KFOR itself being attacked by both sides.

The arrival of NATO forces in Kosovo, the departure of Yugoslav forces and Serbian police, and the imminent return of the Kosova Albanians caused a hurried exodus of much of the non-Albanian population. Revenge attacks by Kosova Albanians—killings, abductions, house burnings—mostly were directed against the Kosovo Serbs and Roma (Gypsies). On the evening of July 23, 1999, fourteen Serb farmers were shot dead as they harvested a field at Gračko, central Kosovo—the biggest single massacre of Serbs since KFOR entered Kosovo. In this chapter, a Serb villager from Gračko relates his experience of that evening.

About half of Kosovo's 200,000 Serbs are now estimated to have left the province. Before the war, approximately 20,000 lived in Prishtina (Priština); now less than 400 remain. Some 150 Serbs currently live with "internationals" in the YU Programme Building under KFOR protection. Other Serbs live in small towns or villages which have become Serb enclaves under KFOR control, such as Gračanica. For the Serbs working as well-paid interpreters for KFOR, OSCE, or the UN, it may be worth putting up with the situation rather than to move to Serbia where they would be lucky to find any work at all.

Many Kosova Albanians perceive the Roma as collaborators. They claim that Roma helped the Serbian paramilitaries, police and Yugoslav Army soldiers to torch houses, bury bodies, steal, and kill. Most of the Roma appear to have left the province but some, like Shemsije, live under KFOR protection in enclaves within towns or villages. Others are in UNHCR camps, like Hashim Berisha, an Ashkali (Albanian-identified Rom), who now lives in confinement near the power station in Obiliq (Obilić) where he used to work. Some Roma manage to live alongside the Kosova Albanians.

During the war, almost all the rural population of Bosniaks (Muslim Slavs speaking the Bosnian language) were forced into exile from Kosovo. After the withdrawal of the Serbian forces and the arrival of KFOR, the urban Bosniak population became targets for attacks by Kosova Albanians. The prewar population of Bosniaks was estimated at 70,000. Now their number is far fewer, though exact figures are hard to obtain.

In Prizren, the Turkish population has remained relatively stable. Although not actively involved in opposing the Serbian regime, Kosovo Turks' sympathies lie with the Albanians, and many Albanians speak Turkish as well as Albanian. The story of a Turkish woman, N., married to an Albanian, appears here.

The climate of fear is such that none of the interviewees wished to be photographed or identified by their full names, with the exception of Hashim Berisha.

A KIND OF PRISON

On July 23, 1999, we started working with combine harvesters in this big field. Twice the combines broke down. I went back to the village at 2:00 P.M. to fix one and then returned at 5:20 P.M. to finish my *ar*.* At 8:30 in the evening, it was dark, but none of the other farm workers had come home, so we called KFOR. We called the base at Lipljan, but Albanian interpreters answered the phone. After the third time that happened, a man from the village traveled to the base and asked the soldiers to come and look for the farm workers. We waited in the village until 2:00 A.M., and then the KFOR soldiers came back. They had found the workers in the field. All fourteen were dead. They took the bodies to Priština hospital. None of the Albanian terrorists were found. Afterward, we went to the field. The farm machinery was all over the place—a tractor here, a combine there. There was blood and brains everywhere. There was a crowbar lying on the ground.

We never expected something like this to happen. We thought we were safe in a group. Many of the workers weren't even farmers, they were just helping with the harvest. None of us had any connection with the paramilitaries. If we had done something bad to the Albanians, we would have expected retaliation, and we would have brought our guns to protect ourselves. But we'd never harmed them. We weren't expecting anything.

We never had trouble in this village before. There are only three Albanian families in the village, and we never had problems with them. But now we have no contact—they never said they were sorry. Nobody wants to work here anymore.

Serb villager, age 40
Gračko (Graçkë), April 28, 2000

* Serbian, a measure of land ten meters by ten meters

My family moved to Kosovo from Novi Pazar in Sandžak when I was sixteen. My husband died thirty-five years ago. I live here with my fifty-six-year-old daughter.

Every day we expect someone to come and kill us. We didn't used to have problems with the Albanians, but now it's too dangerous even to speak Serbian on the street. Twice last June, Albanians threw grenades into our garden. We haven't been on the street for the past eight months. When we went out last summer, Albanian women and kids shouted abuse at us and threw rubbish at us. When I went to the market, an Albanian trader said, "Don't speak Serbian to me—we don't use the Serbian language anymore, it's finished. I'm not selling to you." That was the last time I went out shopping. In July, all we ate was bread. In August, KFOR began protecting us and brought us food packages from the UNHCR. Later we received food aid.

We don't go into the garden unless KFOR is here. They come round every two hours; two soldiers sleep here three nights a week. Without them, we would be dead. Last autumn, an Albanian climbed up onto our roof and tried to get in. A woman banged on our door with an iron bar and shouted, "I'll kill you!" It's always at night, so we never see their faces. Once, an Albanian interpreter was accompanying KFOR soldiers, and he told us to leave Kosovo and go to Serbia—but the soldiers couldn't understand what was being said.

We used to be good neighbors with one Albanian family. Now Albanians are afraid to speak to us. We don't know why they hate us. We don't know anything. We have our own troubles and know nothing about politics; I mind my own business. Nobody expelled the Albanians. They left because of the bombs and went to Albania or Macedonia.

We have no family, and our three Serb neighbors have left. We've never had a telephone; neither our television nor our radio works, and we never see newspapers. Sometimes the power cuts last for three days. Every day we live in this terrible silence.

L., age 76, Serb

Priština (Prishtina), February 17, 2000

In September, 2000, the women sold their house to an Albanian family and moved to Niš, Serbia.

We've lived here since 1957. Our friends were from every ethnic group—Turks, Albanians, Bosniaks, and Serbs. I was a tax inspector, and my wife worked in a bank for twenty-two years. My wife's ancestors have lived in Prizren since 1770.

In 1998, some Serbs were kidnapped, and we were all fearful. After the bombing last year, our Albanian friends continued to visit us in our house, but once we had KFOR protection, they came by less often because KLA monitors were based in the house opposite. Now we only see our Albanian friends late at night, because they're afraid to be seen visiting us.

The first ten days after NATO arrived, we had no problems, but then Albanians who don't know us moved from their villages into houses close by, and soon we were the only Serbs living on the street. We were very frightened, especially at night. We were constantly watching out of the windows, hearing threats and shouts outside. Then KFOR hired my daughter as a Serbian interpreter, and now, because of her, we have good KFOR protection. We've sent the younger children to Belgrade for safety. KFOR soldiers sleep here every night and give us twenty-four-hour security. Last September, a bomb was thrown into our house while we were playing cards with the KFOR soldiers. It exploded and damaged the kitchen, but nobody was hurt. A few weeks ago, KFOR caught two Albanians climbing up onto our roof.

I have heard about the massacres of Albanians from Albanian friends and from Radio Free Europe, but I didn't see anything. Some stories may be exaggerated or not true. I have seen many houses destroyed by Serbs, but I wonder when the Albanians will understand *our* situation. This is the second time that Albanians have thrown us out of Kosovo. In 1940, my whole family had to find refuge in Montenegro. It was only thanks to *honest* Albanians that we weren't killed.

I've only been on the street, with KFOR escort, three times in the past nine months; my wife came out only once. When my mother-in-law went shopping with KFOR, Albanian villagers shouted abuse at her: "Go to Serbia," "This [Kosovo] is not yours," "We are going to kill you." She hasn't gone out shopping since. I miss my work and my freedom. My wife keeps sane by reading a good deal—classics by Tolstoy, Dostoyevsky, Stendhal. I spend a lot of time in my workshop, in the part of the garden which isn't visible from the street. I feel very uncomfortable when I go out the front door. Sometimes I see an Albanian friend pass by. Our eyes meet for a moment, and I can't see any animosity, but we can't speak because it's dangerous for him.

Every day we receive phone calls from Serb friends in Serbia, asking us if it's safe for them to come back to Prizren. I tell them they know better than we do—we have little information. Of course we are optimistic; we want to stay because

Prizren is our home. If we went to Serbia, we would have no work, nothing. I've done twenty years' volunteer work for the Red Cross, and I can't imagine myself waiting in a queue as a refugee.

I.S., age 45, Serb
Prizren, April 25, 2000

When I returned to the house in October, 2000, only Mr. S's mother-in-law remained. On April 26, the day after this interview, the couple left to join their children in Belgrade.

I was born here in Gračanica, and I married Vladimir in the monastery in 1975. At my wedding, I had guests of many ethnicities. Vladimir was godfather to an Albanian colleague's children.

Through the 1980s, our freedom was reduced bit by bit—there were incidents of Serb children being stoned and Serb girls being raped by Albanians in mixed towns and villages. Our papers reported the rapes regularly, but nobody in the outside world was interested in what was happening to the Serbs. The Albanians were the majority in the Kosovo government, and usually none of the rapists were caught. We didn't trust the legal system, how could we? From 1990 onward, we felt a bit freer because Serbia sent more police down to Kosovo. The Albanians had real reasons to be fearful because they didn't respect the law. Life was normal until 1998, when traveling once again became risky. The Albanians felt that the Serbian police were occupying them.

I remember going to Priština in 1982 to visit a friend. That evening, during the *korzo*, I saw the Albanians walking on one side and the Serbs on the other. My Albanian friend and I walked in the middle of the street. In the shops though, nobody cared about your ethnicity—business was business.

During the NATO bombing last year, I asked my friend, "Why are you leaving?" and she said, "All my people are going; I have to go." I asked, "Did someone push you to leave?" and she said, "If I don't go, other Albanians will think I am a traitor." She telephoned me from Macedonia in June 1999 and said, "If I could return home just for one moment, nobody could push out me until I die." She advised us not to leave Kosovo. This was the last time I heard from her. The phones in Gračanica only work within the village. I'd like to see her again, but she fears her own people too much to have contact with us. Now the Albanians are faced with their own terrorists, as we were, terrorists among themselves, needing money, apartments, cars. Now KFOR is arresting more Albanians than Serbs. I don't believe in the "massacres" of Albanians during the war. Massacres aren't in the Serbian tradition. Only two thousand five hundred bodies have been found so far, so the figures have been exaggerated.

Albanians hate everything that is Serbian. This war is not a religious war. It has nothing to do with Muslim/Christian differences, although large families are connected with religion—to be a true Albanian, every Albanian woman had to bear six children. The Albanians' only weapon was to have too many kids.

After KFOR arrived in Kosovo, I stopped going to Priština. I don't go out of Gračanica anymore, and I feel claustrophobic. I am trying not to notice KFOR here; why should they need to protect us in our own country? We'd be safer with

Serbian police, but I don't know if that day will ever come. I could live with Albanians if there was no violence, but I would lose my identity if I lived in an Albanian state. If Kosovo becomes independent, I will be a foreigner in my country.

Gradimirka, age 44, Serb
Gračanica (Ulkian), February 15, 2000

We always used to eat together from one dish—Albanians, Roma, Ashkalia—in my home, in the army, in the brick factory, and on the construction site. I've had Albanian friends for twenty-six years and I cannot forget them. They never made food for Ramadan without inviting me. When my father died, they came to pay their respects, as did my Serb friends. It was normal, we worked together.

Our friendships with Albanians changed only after NATO's arrival in June. I went to see an Albanian friend who had just returned from abroad. He said, "I don't want to talk to you because you killed my people, you killed children." I had known him since we were kids.

An Albanian neighbor came inside my home with his shoes on; this was a terrible moment, as it goes against our custom. It was on June 22, last year; he wanted to check that none of his stolen possessions were in my house. Only a few weeks earlier, we had greeted each other on the street. He examined my TV, the video, everything. I warned him to be careful of my dog because he could get bitten. I told him, "You can check my house, but you can't touch my dog." He said, "I can kill your dog if I like." Then this guy's brother tried to go into my brother's house, but another Albanian, I think from the KLA, pointed his gun at him and said, "You can't loot this house, because the owner looked after my house during the war, and he isn't guilty. I know for certain he didn't steal anything."

During the bombing, I worked as a manual worker in Kosova A. My Roma and Ashkalia friends told me, "Soon we will not find Serbs or Ashkalia or Roma here. It will be ethnically clean, just Albanians." On June 28, two KLA soldiers came to our street in Obiliq and asked if we had had anyone serving in the Serbian army. We said no. "OK, you can stay," they said. "Give up your guns, and you can carry on living here." Two or three days afterward, the street was filled with armed Albanians who told us to get out of our homes. "You have no place here," they said, "We will burn your houses." Within two days, the Ashkalia and Roma decided to leave together, and we went by tractor to Fushë Kosovë, six kilometers away.

The Albanians watched us as we left, and afterward I heard they had been inside our houses. Three or four weeks later, my son went near our home to see what had happened. The windows and door of our house had been taken, and the roof had been removed. They took everything they needed, and later they burned the house. I've seen the burned out shell.

We've been in this camp in Plemetin since December 1999, and before that in a camp near my house in Obiliq. We are not criminals—but we are in jail. There isn't enough food in the camp. We used to get a chicken leg once a week; now it's every three weeks. We receive flour, vegetable oil, beans, and rice. We don't have any cigarettes or *rakia*, so some people sell their food rations to get money. But we feel loved by the Italians and Albanians who work here. Lorenz, an

Italian aid worker, bought me medicine for my high blood pressure. We have a carpentry workshop, and I am making tables. Work gives my life meaning.

I never expected this to happen, and I am very angry with the Albanians. It's not right that we should all carry the guilt for crimes committed by individuals. There is no proof that my family did anything. I didn't see anyone collaborating with the Serbs. If some Roma or Ashkalia collaborated with Serbs, then they should be charged. I don't know if anyone here in the camp is guilty.

Hashim Berisha, age 52, Ashkali
Plemetin (Plementina) camp, near Obiliq (Obilić), May 2, 2000

In January 1998, I lost my job because of my politics and my ethnicity. I was against the regime, and an activist in the local Bosniak party. A Serb woman was employed in my place—the Serbs numbered 7 percent of the citizens in Prizren, but they controlled 93 percent of the population.

Fear was our permanent escort from early 1998. The Albanians were the main focus of harassment, but we didn't talk to them much; they didn't trust us—each community had kept fairly separate for the last ten years. I had some Albanian acquaintances, but my closest friends were Bosniak. We met in both Serb and Albanian cafés, but we weren't trusted by either side. The last Bosniak café closed in April 2000—we were worried that Albanian groups might throw grenades through the window. Before the war, it was the Serbs who broke the windows of the cafés; after the war, it was the Albanians. So for the last few months we've been to mostly Albanian cafés.

During the NATO bombing, many of us fled Prizren for the Bosniak villages of the Župa valley. On May 1, 1999, probably by mistake, NATO bombed Jablanica, one of our villages. Two were killed, sixteen injured, and many houses and the mosque were damaged. My wife, kids, and I fled to Bosnia and stayed with friends in Sarajevo. Life wasn't easy there. I used to read, listen to the radio news, and walk past all the ruined buildings. I thought about survival. I felt stupid. I told myself I should have left Kosovo earlier. I was worried about friends and relatives still in Prizren. In Sarajevo, newspapers were very expensive and secondhand books were cheaper—so I bought books rather than newspapers. I bought a Larousse encyclopedia, novels by Yugoslav writers such as Ivo Andrić, Meša Selimović, Dobrica Ćosić, Ćamil Sijarić, and classics by Tolstoy and Dostoyevsky. Now it's very difficult for us to find books and newspapers in our language here in Prizren.

When I crossed the border back into Kosovo on July 25, 1999, I felt reborn. Back in Prizren, our house was still OK, but we didn't feel safe—young Albanians were shooting in the air and throwing stones into our courtyard. We asked for protection from the German KFOR, but I think they saw us in the same bracket as the Serbs. The world sees Albanians as good, Serbs as bad, and doesn't even know about us—it may be that our language links us with Serbs. The Turkish KFOR soldiers are the only ones who try to be fair to all ethnic groups.

After the war, some fifty thousand Albanian refugees from the villages arrived in Prizren; most of them had never heard our language. We had no freedom of speech. At the mosque we all—Albanians, Bosniaks and Turks—prayed together with no problem, but when I saw a friend on the street, we used sign language or waved, we never spoke. I had the urge to scream sometimes, to speak loudly in my own language in the street.

Things are better now—the Albanians know the Serbs are gone, and they are beginning to recognize our dialect. I am also trying to improve my Albanian. I think Prizren will be multi-ethnic again—but not the rest of Kosovo.

One night in early January 2000, a Bosniak family was murdered in the Tusus neighborhood of Prizren, the first time in the history of the Prizren Bosniaks that a whole family was massacred. Unlike the Albanians and the Serbs, we don't like using guns or even seeing guns. We are a pacifist community. They built myths around arms, fighting, and struggle; we have a history of

living peacefully. We don't mind who is in power; we know *we* won't be in power. After the massacre, we wondered, "Who's next?" It affected all of us.

I have no work. The whole family has no source of income and is surviving on loans from relatives. If there was a chance to leave for a Western country, I would go tomorrow. We Bosniaks will always be in the minority. With each new regime, we face new hardships. We are like Sisyphus in the Greek myth, pushing the stone up the mountain in vain.

M.B., middle-aged, Bosniak
Prizren, October 19, 2000

I was born in Dardania, in Priština. The Albanians killed my father in front of our block on June 20, 1999. He was fifty and a locksmith—he'd never been in the army or the police. My mother was pregnant with my sister. Six days after the death of my father, Irish KFOR soldiers came to live in our flat. They stayed until December. When they couldn't guarantee our safety anymore, they told us to move here. We were the last Serb family to leave the block. For five months, I didn't go out on the balcony or even look through the window because Albanians were throwing stones and breaking the glass and calling us names.

I used to have at least thirty Albanian friends—we used to go to the same primary school, in different classes. I had no problems with the Albanians—no fights, nothing. The Albanians would talk to me in Serbian, and some of the Serb kids spoke Albanian. I understand Albanian but can't speak it very well. Sometimes we would play together outside on our block until midnight. My very best friend was an Albanian boy.

In November, my Albanian friend came to our apartment block and asked for me in Serbian. I came downstairs to see him. We only talked for five minutes because we were afraid that other Albanians would see us. He's half Albanian and half Turkish, and he was having problems, too. Three days before he visited me, Albanians had knocked his Turkish father to the ground and beaten him. So he told me to look after myself and to be on my guard all the time. I haven't seen him since then. I still trust him, but my mum doesn't.

At the moment, I'm the only pupil from the YU Programme Building to go to school in Laplje Selo, and I have to go in a UN police car. Sometimes I have to wait for them outside our block—if they're late, I get scared. Somebody once threw a bottle at me; another time, someone threw eggs. Two days ago, KFOR placed a soldier on guard there.

Milorad, age 16, Serb

Priština, (Prishtina), February 16, 2001

I was working in Tuzla, Bosnia. During the Bosnian war, we had to leave everything and flee from Tuzla with just one bag of clothes. My wife Cvetanka and I eventually moved back to Kosovo, where I found work in the Dobro Selo coal mine near Obilić. In the summer of 1994, we moved to our current flat in Priština in the YU Building. Now we live under KFOR protection.

I always had excellent relationships with Albanians. I had around ten close Albanian friends. Now two of my former Albanian colleagues come here to visit me at night—when it's safer for them. The first visit was last November. One evening, I came back from shopping in Gračanica, and as I arrived at my building, a man called out to me, but I couldn't see who it was. "It's me, it's me," he said and gave his name in Albanian. I looked everywhere and saw him hiding in the dark under the walkway. I was very surprised, but he was even more surprised to see me still alive. It was very nice, he was a real friend. After that, he would visit me, but just for a few minutes at a time. It wasn't safe for him to stay long.

My other Albanian visitor used to work at the mine, but we hadn't met before the war. Our mining company used to work in cooperation with a German company, so after the war, my former German colleagues asked this man to find out if I was OK. He telephoned me and asked, "Do you need anything? Do you need food, money?" He said he would visit me and told me the color of his car—he couldn't give me a license plate number because most cars after the war had no license plates. I didn't feel scared—why should I? It was dangerous for him, not for me. I waited for him in the rain, at dusk, and then I saw him get out of the car. He was wearing the overcoat he had described, with the company logo stuck on his left pocket. We couldn't speak Serbian on the street, of course, but we spoke Serbian inside the flat. In December, when the Kosovo B power station broke down, the Germans asked him to see if I could help fix it. He came with technical questions I tried to answer. He's been here three times in the past year. His visits are brief—just long enough for coffee and brandy.

We Serbs are living in a big prison. We never go out except for weekly shopping in Gračanica with a KFOR escort. So many of us in the YU Programme Building are under lots of stress, physical and psychological—the worst is boredom, having no job. I feel very tired. I am teaching myself English and reading Jules Verne's *Around the World in Eighty Days*. I want to improve my Albanian. I understood enough Albanian for my job in the mine, and I speak a little.... But I already speak Russian and German—and, after all, we still live in Serbia.

I never liked Milošević, but I know that the Serbs did not make war in Bosnia and Croatia. It's a big lie, and all the Muslim people in Bosnia know that. The massacres in Kosovo? Also a lie, in my opinion. I know that innocent people were killed in the war, and I know from TV that NATO bombs may have killed more than a hundred people. It is possible some massacres happened, but to say that they took place before the bombing is not true, really that is not true.

I think that the Albanian people are under a great pressure to conform. Same thing with Serbs—if I hear a Serb say all Albanians are bad, that Serb is not thinking for himself. Albanians have been taught to hate; it is their illness. If they thought for themselves, I think many would think like me. It's good that Rugova won the local elections, that's a big step.

Two months ago stones were thrown at our windows at night. A week ago there was a rocket-propelled grenade attack on our block and one apartment was damaged. Tonight, an Albanian man was working outside the building. I asked him in Albanian, "Are you tired?" He shook his spade, "I will show you how tired I am." My wife and I went inside and said to each other, "He didn't reply, 'How are you?' He was rude." We're a bit shaken up by that.

Miroslav, age 62, Serb
Priština (Prishtina), October 31, 2000

I was born in Prizren and married an Albanian in 1974, when there were many mixed marriages. Nobody cared about ethnicity then—maybe we just didn't notice it.

During the 1990s, when the schools were closed to Albanian pupils, I kept my job as a Turkish teacher. I loved my school and my students. I put on a mask to survive. I was good friends with my Serb colleagues. I shared personal secrets with them that I wouldn't tell my sisters. I haven't seen them since I was finally forced to leave. I was trying to stay away from politics, but it was very hard living in two different communities.

At the beginning of April last year, Serbian paramilitaries came to our neighborhood. We escaped to my mother's house, but a week later we came back, early in the morning. My husband went right to work, and I started cleaning. I was having a cup of tea, when all of a sudden I heard noises. I peeped out of my window and saw a group of at least twenty paramilitaries. They banged loudly on our door. My husband arrived a few moments later. I had just prepared his breakfast. Three months later, when we returned, the same tea was in the pot, moldy. The table was the same as when I had left—olives, white cheese, red pepper paste, and bread.

The paramilitaries rushed into the yard with their guns. They weren't wearing masks, and I knew them all. There was an ex-pupil of mine, a civilian with a gun. I grabbed his face and asked, "Why are you doing this to me? Don't you know me?" He said, "Of course I know you, you were my teacher, but we've been ordered to do this." Today, I want to see them again and ask, "Why did you do this?"

Two of the policemen were sweating. They knew us well. They searched every corner of the house—in every cigarette pack, under every bed. I wanted to say so many things, but I became tongue-tied. They took all our savings, our valuables, our photo albums, documents, the cordless phone (our youngest son's favorite thing), pens, cigarettes, even our tissues. They were saying, "You have all these things, but the soldiers don't." They made my husband carry it all out to their truck. "What were you teaching in the school?" they asked me. "Were you teaching students how to use guns?"

They told us to leave in twenty minutes, and we thought they meant leave the house. So we hid at my sister-in-law's place that night, and then my husband went to work the next morning. A paramilitary noticed him and pointed a gun at him, "What did I tell you? You must leave Kosovo. You have twenty minutes to leave Kosovo A and go to Kosovo B…"* We went to Albania.

* *"Kosovo B" is a sarcastic reference to Albania.*

We had great dreams about life—we had money. We were going to build a big house. When I see other people's big houses being built now, I feel jealous. I sleep at the most three hours a night, despite taking sedatives and antidepressants. I am obsessed with what happened. It was so terrible to be a refugee, sleeping in Tirana in the same clothes day after day. I still have my coat—maybe it will speak one day.

I cry constantly; I cannot find myself in myself. I used to write easily—poetry, prose—but that time has passed. I still teach, and my students love me, but I don't enjoy it anymore.

I feel better since I met Semih in March.[*] I used to see the NGOs and their cars everywhere and think, "What are they doing here? What use are they?" I feel embarrassed about that now because of my friendship with Semih. He's the only one who listens to me and who makes me happy.

My husband moves in the outside world, but I don't. Women don't go out in my culture: I have not been out with my female friends more than four or five times in my whole life. Recently, I asked my son, "Let me have one day out with you," but he said, "I don't go out with my mother on the street."

N., age 48, Turk
Prizren, April 24, 2000

[*] *Semih Bülbül, Community Services Officer for UNHCR.*

I've always experienced discrimination—verbal abuse and teasing about my dark skin. We have Albanian names and we speak Albanian on the street, but we speak Romany inside the house. We are just three women here, and we are Muslim. We used to go to the mosque with the Albanians, for Bajram or Ramadan, but not since the war began. When we sold clothes in the market, we always shared our food with other traders, both Albanians and Serbs. We used to travel to Turkey every week to buy clothes, but I had to stop my trips in 1998.

For a week in the summer of 1998, while KLA soldiers fought for control of Rahovec, we stayed inside. When the situation quieted down a bit, the Serbs accused us of protecting the Albanians with snipers. During the NATO bombing in 1999, we hid in a cellar in our brother's house. The paramilitaries, Yugoslav army soldiers and police, killed two hundred to three hundred people in Rahovec, including the Imam. Some of the Serbs were darker skinned than I, and that's why the Albanians now think some Roma here were involved in the war. The Serbs also forced Roma people to open graves and to steal animals.

When NATO came into Kosova, we hugged each other in the street. We went into town to buy cigarettes. A KLA soldier came up to me and asked, "Why are you out in the street? Your place is in Serbia"—and he took the cigarettes. The cigarette seller, who knew me, was red in the face, but the KLA soldier was armed. I said, "You can push me out when I am dead. I'm not moving from here!" My sister and sister-in-law had to force me back home.

Soon after this incident, Albanians began to beat and kidnap Roma people. In late June 1999, Shkelzen, Tasim, Masllum, and Isuf disappeared from our neighborhood. Back in 1998, Azem, Visar, and Agron had been taken by the KLA. We've had no news at all about them.

I only can go into town in an OSCE car. If we get out of the car and walk on the street, Albanians say to us, "You won't always have KFOR to protect you!" My sister goes to town about once a month. She is not scared like I am. She even jokes with me that I must have done something to feel so afraid! But if I go out and someone accuses me of stealing or killing, I know I will explode.

We sometimes see Albanians walking past to visit old Serbian friends. We talk with them on the street, and they say that we'll all live together again.

It's a lie that we are together with the Serbs. In the Serb time, the Serbs never liked us. Our Serb neighbors used to say, "You are like Muslims, you're like the Albanians," because my mother wears a headscarf. We identified with the Albanians. When I saw on TV how they were being pushed out, I cried for them. Now I am happy they are free, but what about us? They should punish those who committed the crimes and give us back our freedom.

My uncle comes here to visit us on the bus from Gjakovë and he has no problem—the Roma are treated better in Gjakovë; they can work. Roma go to mixed weddings and to cafés there—and apparently there is even more freedom in Prizren. I know of some Roma living near the hospital here who have good relations with Albanian families, and I also know that the white-skinned Roma are going out more. But we are dark skinned, and we live very close to the Serbs.

In September 1999, several of us started a women's group with the help of the Albanian organization Motrat Qiriazi. We get together for tea and coffee and listen to music, and we have literacy and sewing classes. I've been to some women's meetings in Gjakovë, Pejë, Prishtina and Ohrid—Albanians, Bosniaks, Goranis, and Roma together—and they were really good. The meetings give me hope, and I feel good about myself. I went to a Roma gathering in Macedonia and made new friends there. For a while, I forgot the war, and I felt liked. I hadn't felt liked in a long time.

Shemsije, age 27, Romni
Rahovec (Orahovac), February 14, 2001

As I traveled around the province in the spring of 2000, I was moved by the way the landscape had been changed by war. A dot of red, an Albanian flag, waving in the breeze beyond bright green barley, marked the graveyard where Raza Elezi's sons are buried. Wreaths wrapped in plastic by a roadside commemorated the anniversary of the NATO bombing of a bus crossing the bridge at Lluzhan (Lužane). This landscape bears witness to countless stories of loss, bereavement, and narrow escapes from death.

Throughout Kosovo, snapshots of the missing and the dead are wedged into the edges of picture frames, tucked inside wallets, and framed under glass to be brought out at demonstrations. I met Nafije Bërbatovci at a demonstration for the missing in Prishtina (Priština) in October 2000. I was moved by how she held onto a tiny sliver of a photograph of her husband. I met Mustafë Musa by chance on the Lluzhan bridge on May 2, 2000, the day after the anniversary of the NATO bombing. A thunderstorm broke, and we took shelter in a car where he told me how his daughter and his niece had died on that bus a year earlier.

An interpreter in Prizren introduced me to Zurija, a Gorani woman from Dragash (Dragaš), a town in the mountains near the borders with Macedonia and Albania. Her husband is missing. Most Goranis (literally *mountaineers*) consider themselves Muslim Slavs. During the Kosovo conflict, some Gorani politicians supported the Serb position—this led to distrust on the part of Kosova Albanians. However, Goranis and Kosova Albanians did not take up arms against each other, and local Gorani police often saved Albanian houses from being burned by Serbian police. Despite willingness by Goranis to coexist with Kosova Albanians, high unemployment and sporadic grenade attacks on apartment blocks in the town of Dragash have contributed to an exodus of the Gorani community. About 1,500 Goranis remain in Dragash: the rest live in villages in the Gora region. The total Gorani community in Kosovo currently fluctuates between 9,000 and 11,000. Goranis also live in Macedonia and Albania.

It is difficult to ascertain the exact number of people who are missing, especially since families do not all report their missing relatives to the same agency. The International Committee of the Red Cross (ICRC) lists 3,525 people missing from all ethnic groups. These are people who were reported missing between January 1998 and April 2001. They include 2,746 Kosova Albanians, 516 Serbs, 137 Roma. Montenegrins, Bosniaks, Goranis, Turks, and Macedonians account for the remaining 126.

I first heard the saying "Death is closer than the shirt you are wearing" in Albanian: "Më afër vdekja se këmisha veshur." Later I learned it also existed in Turkish ("Ölüm yakadan daha yakındır") and in Serbian ("Smrt je bliža od kragne") as "Death is closer than your shirt collar."

DEATH IS CLOSER THAN
THE SHIRT YOU ARE WEARING

I moved to Gllogovc in 1961 when I married Hamzi. My husband and my four brothers-in-law all spoke Serbian and socialized with our neighbors. We had Serb friends in those days and Serb guests at our wedding.

Our problems started in the late 1960s. We had bought a shop, worked very hard, and were better off. There were fights because Serbs would come into the shop and not pay for goods, or Serbian police would come and say the food had expired. At that time, many Serbs sold their land and their houses and moved out of Kosova.

Beginning in 1981, the Serbs closed Albanian shops. The state ordered the land to be divided, giving Albanian land to the Serbs. My husband was jailed several times because he was trying to stop the Serbs from building on his land—eventually he had to give the land up.

In 1998, the war started nearby in Drenica. That August, the police accused my eldest son Ismet of working with the KLA. They beat him for five days; his hands were sore for weeks. Our cousins had been helping wounded KLA soldiers in a clinic, but Ismet had nothing to do with the KLA. After the beatings, he and his younger brother Bekim fled to their wives' family in Vërbovc.

On the night of April 29, 1999, NATO bombed the Feronikl plant, which had been used as a police base. The very next morning, Serbian police surrounded Vërbovc, divided the women from the men, told the women to go to Gllogovc, and killed all the men. We didn't know they'd been killed until much later. The father of my daughters-in-law disappeared, along with their uncles and cousins, and my two sons.

My daughters-in-law returned to their village with the other women on the following Saturday. When they crossed the bridge, Serbian police asked why so many kids were crying. The women said it was because they were hungry. "No, it's because we've killed their fathers and left their bodies in the mountains." Once again, they sent the women to Gllogovc. The women returned to the village the next day. A surviving neighbor told them what had happened to the men, but he could not say if our husbands and sons were among the dead. On May 4, paramilitaries came and ordered us out of our house, and we fled to Macedonia.

Meanwhile, my daughter in Germany found out on the Internet the names of all those massacred, and told our cousin, who was documenting the deaths back in Kosova. But he deliberately didn't list the names of my two sons—he didn't want the family to find out in this way. I only found out fifteen days later, when my daughter rang me in Macedonia. I kept the news to myself—I didn't tell my daughters-in-law until we came home to Kosova at the end of June.

We were told thirteen men had been caught and tortured before they were shot with their hands tied behind their backs. But our cousin said our men were shot from a distance, that they were shot as they were trying to run away. He buried them together in one grave. Weeks later, KFOR and people from The Hague tribunal exhumed the bodies and we buried them properly.

I still can't think of my two boys as dead. I keep thinking if only they could have felt this freedom we feel now, just once. The sorrow goes away slowly, very slowly. I keep wanting to talk to my relatives about them, but I worry I am burdening them. Ismet and Bekim each had three young children, and I feel so sad for them and for my daughters-in-law. If it wasn't for the children, what would we do? Everybody feels the loss. Even now, people still ask for Ismet and Bekim when they come into the shop after returning from abroad.

How many generations will have to pass before we can forget? There were so many killed. I don't ever want to see a Serb near me, civilian or soldier, even the Serbs who are not to blame—and they are a small number.

What happened to us was retaliation for NATO bombing, but we do not blame NATO. We expected retaliation, and if they hadn't bombed it would have been even worse. If I had had a gun during those days of the war, I would have joined the KLA myself.

Raza Elezi, age 57, Albanian
Gllogovc (Glogovac), April 21, 2000

We've been married for thirty-six years, and my husband Rrahim is now almost sixty. We had good relationships with the Serbs up until ten years ago. My husband was a ticket collector. He spoke good Serbian, worked together with Serbs on the train, and used to travel up to Belgrade and back. He was never afraid, never felt in danger until the morning of March 27, 1999. That morning, I asked him why he bothered going to work, as I thought there wouldn't be any buses [to the railway station at Fushë Kosovë]—NATO had started bombing three days earlier.

But there was a bus. We heard that masked paramilitaries got on and that five male passengers were forced to leave. My husband should have come home at 3:00 P.M., but he never came back. We waited the next day and the next.

After two weeks of the bombing, we were forced out by VJ soldiers and Serbian paramilitaries and fled to Albania. We returned in July to find both our houses burned. We lost everything, all our clothes, our photo albums. But we have one photo of my husband, which was taken in a studio a few years ago because he wanted to be photographed with our eldest son, Ibrahim. My daughter kept this photo with her while we were refugees in Albania. Rrahim was wearing the uniform in the photo when he left for work the day he disappeared.

We have searched the mass graves and the clothing found by The Hague tribunal. We went to look at the mass grave discovered recently in Dragodan where they found two of our neighbors among the bodies. We have been to the Red Cross regularly and reported to the new office for missing persons, but there's no news. It's been eighteen months now, and as each day passes, we feel worse.

We can't forget him even for one minute. I spend every day imprisoned in this house, because even if I go somewhere I can't leave the sadness behind. We watch every single news program. We just want to hear something about him. I take tranquilizers regularly, but each time a mass grave is opened, I can't sleep and I can't eat for a week—I am so afraid we will find him.

Nafije Bërbatovci, age 58, Albanian
Miradi e Ulet, October 17, 2000

One night in November 1998, I drove my sister back to her home in Podujevë, and on the way, I was waved into our petrol station by a group of seventeen Serbian policemen. They told me to turn off my lights, open the boot, and accused me of not having a permit for my first aid kit—which, of course, was rubbish. They ordered me to drive my car into a field. I knew they would kill me there. I started driving but then refused to go any further. One of the policemen yelled at me, but another—who had his car washed at my garage once or twice in the past—persuaded him to let me go.

On December 24, 1998, we woke up to the sound of tanks—the war had arrived in Sekiraçë. The Serbs shot one of my employees as he fled from the petrol station across a field. He crawled through the field, but nobody could reach him because of all the shooting, and he bled to death. After two hours, I went to get his dead body. The Serbs also killed two brothers who live on the other side of the field—they used to supply the KLA with food. And they killed three other civilians in our village. Despite this, I decided to stay. It was better for us all to die than to live under the Serbs.

At the end of March, 1999, the tanks rolled into Sekiraçë. The Serbs shot at us as we fled by car to Batllava. When the Serbs attacked us there, we drove to Koliq, then we ran out of fuel. After two weeks in Koliq, four of us came back to get food from our houses in Sekiraçë. The houses had been ransacked and police were everywhere. I walked twenty-five kilometers through the fields at night with thirty kilograms of sugar, oil, flour, and clothes on my back. We were in Koliq one more week until the shelling started again. In pouring rain, we loaded every-one onto tractors and drove to Prishtina.

As we left Koliq, we saw the injured and dying near the mosque. I saw a shell land right on my friend and blow his legs off. He was killed; many were injured. I saw an old man lying on top of a kid to save him. I'll never forget that sight. All we could do was take six or seven of the injured to the KLA to be treated. We slept in the forest that night.

Next morning, about two hundred men were killed, some by shells, some by gunshots. We ran away. The Serbian police caught up with us and told us we could go back and get our trac-tors—if we paid them. Some men went back, and the Serbs shot them.

In the morning, we arrived in Shajkovc, where there were about a thousand refugees. We slept there two nights and then police said that whoever lived in Sekiraçë could go back as long as we stayed away from the main road. We went back for one night and the shooting began again. That night my son, who had just joined the KLA, saw our big house burn down. My wife and children lived at my cousin's for the next two months.

I lived alone in the small house next to the *oda* for the first two weeks. I occupied myself by painting and decorating, cutting the grass, feeding the hens. The Serbs watched me from the petrol station, but I wasn't afraid. I even slept, I was so used to the fear.

One afternoon, the Serbs made a hole in the wall of the garage and started shooting at me, so I went down to my cousin's place. Then the police moved into my house and killed the chickens—all fifty of them. Our dog was shot dead. One day, I saw a Serb pumping fuel from the tanks in our garage. That night, I took the pumps away from the garage, and that surprised the Serbs in the morning.

The night before NATO came, Serbian tanks arrived. My cousin thought the Serbs were about to attack. We warned everyone to flee. A few hours later, we heard the noise of tanks and thought, "Oh, God, it's the Serbs." We sent a boy up to the roof with binoculars, and he started yelling, "NATO is here!" I said, "I can't wait anymore, I'm going to see NATO!" I crossed the river and saw four NATO soldiers in the distance. I passed through the cemetery and by the house with the Serbian snipers. I looked at the snipers—paramilitaries—and they looked at me. I turned my umbrella to one side so I couldn't see them. I wasn't afraid—I could see NATO tanks in my garage.

I hugged and kissed two English soldiers. We couldn't understand each other, but I know some German. They put up a tent, but I warned them not to go further than the garage because there might be mines. The Serbian police were still living in my house, and the NATO soldiers said they'd be gone by the end of the day.

Outside my house, I saw a jeep and a Serbian guard; to my surprise we said good morning to each other. A Serbian police officer appeared and promised that nothing would be stolen. But after they left the next day, I found that everything was missing—carpets, curtains, even electric switches and cables.

NATO stayed in Sekiraçë for ten days. Afterward, we started clearing out our petrol tanks. The lids had been left open by the Serbs and rain and rubbish had come in. When we started on the second tank, we put a rope down into the petrol, and there was a huge explosion—it was a booby trap.

All I remember is the force of the blast and hot air on my body. I was thrown up into the air and fell ten meters away. When I opened my eyes, I saw the flesh on my hands had been stripped right down to the bone. I had pain in my chest and my skin was burned. My worker was all black from the explosion. Two of my brothers came, put him in the back of the car, and drove us to hospital. I was going crazy from the pain. I was in intensive care, unconscious, for nine days. My assistant died three days later. I have little strength in my hands now. My face was burned, but it's OK now. Sometimes I dream that my hands are on fire, and I leap out of bed. My nine-year-old son, Berat, shares my bed and keeps an eye on me.

I've survived. I got used to it: the stress, the trauma. NATO—and God—saved us (and the KLA!). Every time NATO bombed, I prayed to God to save the pilots. I'm surprised, I never believed NATO would help us. But we have a saying, "It's never too late to do good." All the Serb civilians around here have left. As far as I'm concerned, NATO can stay as long as they like, until there are no Serbs left in Kosova.

Now I feel free. A week ago, I was sitting in my garden. Eight children were playing around me, and I thought, what could be better than this?

Shyqri Ejupi, age 52, Albanian
Sekiraçë (Sekirača), February 14, 1999 and September 29, 1999

Zurija's son

We are from Dragaš, but some in our family lived and worked in Dečani. There were very few Goranis in Dečani, but we never had any problems in our shop and had good relationships with all our customers, Albanians and Serbs. In the 1990s, our politicians began to identify as Goranis, and we lost customers because we worked with the Serbs. We didn't think of ourselves as Goranis—we were Yugoslavs.

Zurija

The first three weeks after the war ended, we had no problems, but then five Albanian neighbors came to my home and asked if we had guns. They said they were from the KLA. My younger son said he would fetch his pistol from his car. When he handed it in to the KLA, one guy said, "You Goranis cannot live here anymore! There is no place for you here." So my son, my daughter-in-law, and their children moved up to the monastery for safety. Serb, Roma, and Albanian civilians were hiding there together with the Serb priests. My husband and I refused to go—we stayed and guarded the house. We were alone and scared, the only Goranis left in Dečani.

Zurija's son

After several weeks of no news, we heard that our parents were in danger. On July 14, my brother and I borrowed a van and drove to Dečani. We went right to the house but saw it burning—nobody was there. We looked everywhere for our parents. An hour later my mother appeared. The house had been looted and set on fire at 5:00 A.M. My father had disappeared. We had arrived too late.

Zurija

There was a KFOR checkpoint two hundred meters from our house. My husband told the soldiers about the fire, but they said they couldn't help us. And so, at 9:00 A.M. he left to report the fire to the KLA—and vanished. Where else could we have gone? The KLA were the authorities, the people in power. I walked around the town in a panic trying to find out what had happened to my husband, but none of my neighbors came out of their houses except for an Albanian woman who made me coffee. I sat on a chair in her courtyard, and she said, "He'll come back," but she knew what had happened to him. I went three times to the KLA, but they wouldn't talk to me. I went to the KFOR checkpoint in front of our shop and asked them to find out if my husband was in the monastery. But he wasn't there. The children around me were screaming, "Serb woman, Serb woman!" I was so confused and upset. KFOR couldn't understand what I was telling them and didn't do anything when an Albanian started to break into our shop—I couldn't explain it was ours.

Zurija's son

When we tried to leave Dečani, the road was blocked by about fifty young Albanian men who stopped our van and demanded we go for "informative talks" at the police station. I asked, "Which police?" They said, "KLA police." They didn't have guns, only a big knife. Two of them got in the car to try to force us to go to the KLA, but just then, a KFOR patrol came by, and my brother hurled himself on top of the jeep. I immediately grabbed one of my brother's kids and threw him into the jeep. The Italian KFOR soldiers didn't understand what was going on. One soldier pointed his gun at me. I shouted, "Terrorists! Bambino!" and put the second child into the jeep. Then KFOR realized what was going on and radioed for help. Soon, reinforcements arrived and the Albanians dispersed. KFOR took us to Peć. They had no idea what it meant to be Gorani, or what had happened to us in Dečani. We finally got an escort home to Dragaš three weeks later.

We are frightened in Dragaš. My mother takes tranquilizers, and my fifteen-year-old son is on antidepressants. I asked an Albanian from Dragaš to go to Dečani to find out what happened to my father—he reported back that my father is dead. I think he has no reason to lie to me. We can never go back to Dečani. We've heard the Goranis are back working in Peć, but here in Dragaš, we cannot work. It would be seen as taking customers from Albanians.

Zurija, age 66, Gorani, and her son, age 43
Dragaš (Dragash), February 11 and 18, 2001

My daughter Drita was an activist, the secretary of the local branch of the LDK and a third-year student of electrical engineering at Prishtina University. Drita was a close friend of the student leader Albin Kurti. During the 1998 student demonstrations in Prishtina, the police were constantly searching for her. She was my oldest girl.

On April 7, 1999, she was forced out of her flat in Prishtina and walked all night to come to Orllan. She brought many refugees with her and fetched milk for the children. She and her seventeen-year-old brother milked cows each morning and collected flour for the thirty thousand refugees on the road, most of them women and children from nearby villages. But after two days, masked policemen came to the house asking for the identity of the one who was helping the refugees.

On April 16, VJ soldiers, police, and paramilitaries forced us to go to Shajkovc. We slept in the forests for two months. The Serbian paramilitaries and police used to take shelter with us, hiding under our plastic sheets from the bombing. They would curse us, "You brought them here— we should have killed you!" We were very scared all the time. We only had bread, sometimes soup, and many children died of starvation. The first night, three or four young kids died right there on the straw from vomiting and diarrhea. We thought we might all die at any minute, surrounded by police, with bullets flying above our heads. I saw one woman literally tearing her hair out in clumps, screaming: "They will kill us!" I tried to calm her down, but I couldn't.

One day the police came into the woods, took all the men, and lined us up. Some were sent by truck to Podujevë, some to Prokuple prison in Serbia; some were beaten and then came back to the forest. They interrogated me but didn't take me. They mostly wanted young men.

Everybody was dehydrated and had very bad diarrhea because the water was polluted. Drita told her mother she and her cousin Fexhrije would go to Prishtina and get medicine from a medical student she knew. I told them not to go because it was dangerous and the police were looking for Drita. She insisted on going to Prishtina, saying that she'd given her word to the people and that she'd die for her country.

There was no bus from Podujevë that day, so Drita and Fexhrije stayed at a friend's house. Then a bus came from Nish, full of paramilitaries. The survivors told us that some of the para-

militaries got out and called the Albanians onto the bus. The Serbs probably suspected NATO would bomb the bus. Some Albanians refused to get on. Others went—it wasn't safe for them but they were desperate to find food.

That same day, from the forest, we saw the bus in flames in the distance on the bridge at Lluzhan. We thought our children had taken the bus the day before. We waited two and a half months before we found out what had happened to them. At first, we thought Drita was in prison. We searched everywhere, asking those coming back from Albania if they had seen her. Some people said they saw her in Macedonia distributing aid, others said she was in prison in Mitrovicë. Why they told us these things, we don't know. In war there is so much misinformation. Then in July 1999, a patient at Prishtina Hospital who had been wounded in the Lluzhan bombing sent someone to tell us that Drita and Fexhrije had also been on the bus and were among the thirty-seven dead. As soon as we heard the news, we all fainted—except for me.

So then I went to the Prishtina morgue. I saw Drita's clothes. I found her notebook, with the details of flour distribution, and I found Fexhrije's necklace. We searched everywhere for their bodies. The Red Cross told us they would help, but nothing ever happened. We asked for help from The Hague tribunal—we have given our blood samples, but we have to wait, maybe for two years. The moment we identify the bodies will be like hearing the news of her death all over again. Our only wish is to find the bones and have a monument erected to her.

I know the bombing was unintentional. But they should at least have come to see us and apologized. As far as I know, no family was visited by NATO. They seem to avoid these kinds of cases.

We returned home from Shajkovc to find everything burned. We slept in the yard under plastic for a month. We expected some aid, but just got a tent. Only 10 percent of Albanians are back in our village, partly because we live only seven kilometers from the border with Serbia, and people are still scared. The Serbs used to have a base here and four hard-line paramilitary families are still living nearby, under KFOR protection, even though they were seen killing.

Drita's books are still in Prishtina. We can't cope with seeing them here. The Hague team is keeping her ID card until the case is resolved. But I keep her student card with me always, in my wallet, next to my heart. My wife looks at Drita's clothes and cries and cries and lets it all out. Every day she goes to Drita's burned out bedroom, and the pain is just as fresh. We don't have her grave, only her room.

I feel sad because Drita never saw Kosova free, as she wanted. Not even for a day. We have memorial meetings in our village, and Drita's sister Shpresa has set up a women's group in Orllan named after her. Drita always wanted her sisters to be as educated as possible, and I am trying to fulfill that promise. Women should have the same rights as men. I always wanted my daughters to be educated and independent. When Drita visited us from Prishtina, we used to talk about political events until midnight. She was my friend as well as my daughter.

Mustafë Musa, age 52, Albanian
Orllan (Orlane), October 14, 2000

In the apartment block where I stayed in Prishtina, I used to hear the sound of Michael Nyman's theme music to the movie *The Piano* drifting up through the plumbing in the bathroom. It took a while to realize that the music was live and that I was living above a young pianist, Linda Kllokoqi. Her views, like those of Alban and Ali Hyseni, interviewed here, were refreshingly different from many I had heard. I was increasingly aware of a large number of Kosova Albanians who rejected the violence committed in their name.

Others were not so optimistic. I spoke with Dragana on my last day in Kosovo in her Serb enclave, near Pejë (Peć). I had hitched a ride from the roadblock to Dragana's house in an UNMIK police car but had to walk back out of the village; the eerie silence of a thick snowstorm emphasized the enclave's isolation. It was a time of high tension—nine days after the bombing of a Serbian bus in a KFOR convoy left eleven people dead and more than forty injured. It was not surprising that her views, like those of many Serbs I met, were less than conciliatory.

As I walked out of the enclave, I thought of Alban, an eighteen-year-old Albanian whom I first saw dancing energetically in a baseball cap in a Prishtina bar. Alban had told me about a Serb woman he had seen on CNN, swearing at Milošević. "She said her family had lived in Kosova for one hundred twenty years and that 'it was because of one person (Milošević) we are in this now.' She said that the Albanians did not deserve what they were put through, but her words were too late." I wondered if indeed her apologies were too late. As this book goes to press, evidence of massacres committed by Serb soldiers are just beginning to appear in the Belgrade media, and reconciliation between the Serbs and Albanians may be a small step closer.

The book ends with the words of Ali Hyseni, whom I first met six years ago. Hyseni lives in the same house in Kosovo where I interviewed him for *Homes and Gardens* (Chapter 1, page 13), but now he can be photographed on his own land and allow his name to appear in print.

PAST PRESENT IN TIME FUTURE

Before the war, I was arrested twice by the Serbian police. First, because I was wearing black trousers and a red shirt. We Albanians knew it was dangerous to wear red and black together, and I was the only one in the school to do so. The police asked, "Which state are you living in?" I answered, "Kosovo." They threatened to hit me, so eventually I said, "Yugoslavia." They wanted me to say, "Serbia." They warned me, "If you wear the flag colors again, you will have problems with us."

Early in 1998, I was arrested a second time as I returned from a party with three friends. The policemen taunted us, "Why are you going to parties when your brothers in Drenica are dying?" I said, "I'm too young. I don't think about politics." But when I got home, I thought it's true what they say about our brothers dying in Drenica. Here we are, every night on CNN, seeing pictures of houses burning only twenty to thirty kilometers away. I thought of joining the KLA—I think very highly of them—but I'm a pacifist and I supported Rugova. I thought he would keep the peace.

Even in early 1999, my friends at school carried on, making jokes and laughing, "Oh, we're sick of politics, let's have fun!" I was sad and frustrated because nobody, not even my teachers, wanted to discuss what was happening. My father was the only one I could talk to. Every day after school, I used to read plays by Shakespeare to calm down. Then I'd feel better, watch *Euro News* on TV, and hear Kosova called a Serbian province. That would drive me mad.

During the war, we stayed here in Prishtina. I saw people walking down the street, carrying two bags and leaving everything else behind. My father wanted me to leave, but I couldn't convince myself to join them. A group of policemen and soldiers came and ordered us out, but five minutes later, another group arrived and said, "Stay." Three or four times, they gave different orders. The first three weeks, we didn't dare turn on a light. It was like being in prison.

After the war, my friends came back, and some called me a spy. But when we compared how I lived through this time and how they spent their war in Tetovë, Macedonia, going to discos, I felt like some kind of hero for staying here. Many of the people now doing the revenge killings weren't here at all during the war. Now they are back, trying to prove how brave they are.

I could always make the distinction between a people and its regime, and I still do. A whole people cannot be blamed—there were Serbs who felt bad about what was happening to us, like the Women in Black in Belgrade. One day last summer, as Serbs were leaving Kosova, I saw their sad faces looking out of the windows of the KFOR bus, and I thought of my sad face looking out of the window when I was imprisoned in my house during the bombing. Maybe some Serbs deserve this, but not all. I saw this woman on CNN swearing at Milošević. She said her family had lived in Kosova for one hundred twenty years and that "it was because of one person (Milošević) we are in this now." She said that the Albanians did not deserve what they were put through, but her words were too late.

For a long time at school, we were taught that Serbs were the enemy. I believe the Serbs taught the same things to their pupils and encouraged them to kill us. Our generation is not to blame for ethnic hatred. I believe we shouldn't live in the past.

Right now, I'm writing a screenplay for a movie. It's about love, just like in Shakespeare—about forbidden love and the Albanian mentality. Two young people love each other, but each has a different religion: the girl is Muslim and the boy is Catholic. The girl's family condemns their love. I haven't worked out the ending yet.

Alban, age 18, Albanian
Prishtina (Priština), April 18, 2000

We all lived together, Albanians, Turks, and Serbs, with no problems. Local Serbian police officers knew that we were Turks and that there was no trouble in our neighborhood. After the NATO air strikes started in March 1999, the Serbs wanted to force young men like me into their army. I hid in my grandfather's attic. Once, Arkan's men from Serbia came to raid the house next door. I was in the outside toilet at the time, and I was lucky they didn't see me.

At night, my friends and I would jump from one rooftop to another, afraid to go to sleep. When we were in hiding, rats ran all over us, but we couldn't make a single noise, or we'd have been killed. I was reminded of the movie *Rambo II*. When Rambo goes to Vietnam to save his colleagues, he finds prisoners of war imprisoned in a cage with rats running all over them.

One day we were so bored, we went out to play basketball. We thought, if they kill us, so be it—whatever happens, happens. A civilian car came up the street with VJ soldiers inside. Two of my friends ran away. The two of us who stayed were frightened, but the soldiers just took our ball and shot some baskets. Maybe they were jealous and wanted to play, to do something normal, too. Maybe we were just lucky. They chatted with us briefly and admired our hoop. I told them in Serbian how we'd made it.

The Serbs dug a big hole near the sports center and were planning to kill and bury people there. NATO arrived in Prizren just in time. But one of my Turkish friends was killed while working in his uncle's shop, which sold hunting guns.

Two or three days after NATO's arrival, I saw my Serb school friends on the street getting ready to leave Prizren. The Serb mayor of Prizren was saying to the families, "Don't leave, we haven't done anything," but they left anyway. I couldn't talk to them because there were lots of Albanian extremists from the villages around, and they would have said we were collaborating with the Serbs.

Everybody from Prizren speaks Turkish, both Albanians and Turks. But after NATO arrived, many of my friends had problems when they spoke Turkish. The Albanians didn't know that we'd been in hiding, too, and had only eaten bread, salt, and onions for three months.

But since Turkish KFOR has been based here, there's no problem. Everyday I try to improve my Albanian during my work with the Turkish Red Crescent distributing aid to the villages. Now the war seems like a movie. It came and went like the wind. We go out, we date both Albanian and Turkish girls and try to forget the stress.

Yener Gaş, age 19, Turk
Prizren, October 18, 2000

lived all my life in Priština until June 16, 1999, just after NATO entered Kosovo. That day, the Yugoslav Army moved out of the nearby flats and Albanians moved in. The Serbs, Roma, and Turks began to flee to Serbia, Turkey, and Montenegro. There was a big panic heightened by the media, rumors, and gossip. We had no more police.

I wanted to stay in Priština but my father heard that women had been raped by SFOR soldiers in Bosnia and Croatia. And so I moved to Serbia with my brothers, while my parents stayed in Kosovo. During that time, two workers and one professor from my economics school at Priština University were killed by Albanians; an old Serb woman was raped and a neighbor killed. Even though her nephew had been killed in the bombing, my mother could not wear her black mourning headscarf to go shopping for fear of being identified as a Serb. My parents began receiving phone calls from Albanians threatening to kill them. On August 14, 1999, they moved to Medvedja, where we joined them.

In May 2000, I moved to Goraždevac to be near my cousins and to start work with an NGO. I met my fiancé here, in the enclave. It's terrible here. We are eight hundred inhabitants, all Serbian, and we have only two shops and just one café. I am so bored seeing the same people every day—better to stay indoors and read. It's too risky to go out of the enclave.

Goraždevac is surrounded by Albanian villages. In summer 1999, the village was shelled and an old woman was killed; last summer, the village was bombarded with grenades—one person was wounded. I'm not afraid. I'm a good Christian and believe that God will protect me.

I studied economics part time at Priština University and worked as a saleswoman in a Serb-owned furniture store with two Albanian colleagues. I liked individual Albanians—some are good people, but now they are too scared to speak. I miss Shqipe, my good friend. We talked about love and fashion and left politics to the politicians.

The Albanians had a good life; they had fancy cars, luxury furniture. I used to say if they wanted a bigger Albania, they could move to Albania. They would have so many babies that one family member would have to go to Switzerland or Germany to support the rest. They earned money on the black market. Many left their state jobs of their own free will. Repression by the state affected both Albanians and Serbs. The Albanians had TV, radio, and newspapers, and even schools in their own language until 1991, when they left the state secondary schools. They had everything. Before the bombing started, Rugova addressed the Albanians on the radio, telling them to leave for Albania, Macedonia, and Montenegro. The Albanians created the impression that they were forced to leave Priština—it was political manipulation.

As for the massacres, it's not true that Arkan was in Kosovo. There were no paramilitaries in Priština during the bombing.

I don't know about the villages, but I can speak for Priština. My neighbor—an Albanian—was in his flat the whole time and nobody pushed him out. Both sides had criminals wearing masks and stealing, but they weren't paramilitaries. The Albanians are like foxes. They will create mass graves in front of the internationals. This I know, when the Serbian police were here, there were fewer criminals.

Dragana, age 27, Serb
Goraždevac (Gorazhdec), February 25, 2001

My father always warned me because in 1941 his best friend was forced into an oven and burned alive by his Serb friends. He said, "You can never trust people who treat their friends like that." I used to have many Serb friends, but during the war I remembered my father's words.

I started building the bunker in 1986. I built a fence near my house and the bunker beyond it. I told people I was preparing a sports field. Nobody knew what I was doing, not even my family. The bunker was used by the underground resistance movement which had come into being in 1968 but didn't become the official KLA until the 1990s. We stored weapons and documents down there, and people used these weapons to attack police stations. At times, people spent months in the bunker. It had electricity and a toilet. We kept food and water down there. The VJ soldiers came right to the house and never found out.

We knew a week in advance that the Serbs were going to start forcing people out of Prishtina. I asked my KLA people for a round-the-clock guard on our house. By then, we had several thousand refugees from the villages staying in our yard, among the tractors. The people felt safe. We told them we weren't going to let the Serbs come into our compound. On that day, March 29, 1999, we heard shooting in our neighborhood. Some people fled into the fields. My family and others who wanted to stay went into the bunker. An hour later, paramilitaries—Arkan's Tigers—parked three jeeps outside our metal gates, and yelled, "Open up now." We shot at them and killed six immediately—the rest were wounded or took cover. They were not used to resistance and were not expecting any from us. The battle started at 9:00 A.M. The paramilitaries called for reinforcement, and soon they were some one hundred paramilitaries and VJ soldiers with tanks on one side; we were about eighteen or nineteen Albanians, thirteen from my family, on the other. Our family was in the bunker, so we had to fight. Then, at 10:45 P.M., NATO started bombing, and the power went off. The shooting stopped for a bit, and we got our families from the bunker. We told them to join the mass of refugees fleeing Prishtina and never to show their papers because they would be identified as members of this family. By 11:45 P.M., everyone had fled. Our men withdrew and joined the rest of the KLA. Two nights later, I made a satellite call to Germany and found out they were alive in Macedonia. They were one of the first families to get on the trains to Macedonia.

I felt better during the war than now. During the war I used to live in the mountains. I didn't care about TV news, the house, anything. I didn't worry about the family. My one and only goal was to liberate Kosova. Night or day, I had a mission, a military routine. I was in charge of logistics for a brigade of about sixty to seventy KLA men. So I got tired but not psychologically. I felt stronger than I do now. I didn't feel hunger because every day we were fed by the territory we had liberated.

The Serbs who ran from Kosova are now in Belgrade and their situation is even worse than the Albanians' under Serb occupation. One rings me from Belgrade—he cries and weeps for Kosova. He asks, "Do you think we can ever come back?" And I say, "We're working on it" to make him feel better. But as long as this generation is alive, Serbs and Albanians cannot live together.

With each passing day, my impatience is growing, and the consequences of the war are weighing more heavily on me. We won the war, but Kosovars still are not independent. We are now run by the internationals. We have no peace here—because if we had law and order, the internationals would have to go back to their countries and lose their salaries. What kind of security do we have when a man is shot dead in the middle of the day?

These internationals, they come for a six- or twelve-month mission. They don't care about rebuilding this city. For example, some two thousand houses have been built without permits in the city of Prishtina alone. That would have never happened if our own people had been in charge. We could have prevented illegal construction. UNMIK keeps on saying, "We'll look into it," but nothing happens. On the other hand, the Kosova Department of Education wanted to make our burned out house, which we had loaned to an illegal school for years, into a museum, but the internationals refused to issue the permit for it.

I lose patience these days, even with my family. I don't spend time at home. My nerves are shattered and I don't sleep well. I am frustrated and disappointed with UNMIK. I wish the people of Kosova could govern themselves.

Mehmet Aliu, age 54, Albanian
Prishtina (Priština), February 16 and November 1, 2000

Since 1990, I have worked for the Mother Teresa Society, the largest humanitarian organisation in Kosova run by Albanians. In 1998, my distribution of aid for Mother Teresa led to my arrest by Serbian police. I spent seven months in jail, and lost most of the hearing in one ear as a result of brutal beatings. On February 17, 1999, I was tried and thanks to pressure from international agencies, including OSCE and the International Red Cross, I was released.

When I came out of prison I was like a skeleton. I only had one month of freedom before the bombing started. I decided to stay in Gjakovë and witness what was going on. For three months, I only slept one hour every night because I was guarding our house. The Serbs thought I was in Albania; I was on their list to be killed. When I went out shopping, I dressed up like an old woman so as not to be recognized.

One night, April 1, Serbian police and paramilitaries killed seventy people on Sadik Stavileci Street. They suspected that the KLA was there. Twenty women and children hiding in a basement were shot or knifed to death. Their bodies were set on fire. Several of them were my friends.

During the bombing, the paramilitaries and soldiers used heroin and other drugs and raped a lot of women. The women had abortions or the babies were adopted. I decided not to work with women who had been raped—it was just too much for me. But I've had a lot of contact with women in pain, young women who lost their husbands after one or two years of marriage. I opened the Centre for Protection of Women and Children here in Gjakovë, and several widows work there with me—a psychologist, a computer expert, a lawyer, a nurse—together with an economist whose husband is missing. I think the best rehabilitation for traumatized people is to be employed. For widows in the villages, it's very hard to be without men. They have no independence, and no security. Sometimes the widows leave the children with their husbands' families and go back to their own parents.

The NGOs have trained counselors to help with trauma, but the training only lasts a month. Sometimes it's to be good to able to talk, but I have found that going to the place where the massacre took place is most helpful because you are face to face with what really happened, and the pain and sorrow come out.

I long to be alone and cry, but there is no time. I keep it all inside, and it's destructive. I survive for my baby, Leka, whom I adopted in 1998. I'm the first single woman in Kosova to adopt a baby.

Gjakovë is a small town with a lot of sorrow. There have been many protests about our six hundred fifty missing people. But this year, 2001, we are faced with other realities—we have to work and get money. Seventy-five percent of houses and shops were destroyed; half have been rebuilt since autumn. Unemployment is very high, and we desperately need capital—then we won't need food aid.

Thank God the internationals are here because the post-war situation is very difficult. There are so many traumatized people, and some want revenge—and that's very dangerous. They have only tried two war criminals in The Hague. We must show the Albanians that justice is being done, because criminals are still walking around Kosova.

It's too soon for reconciliation. The politicians and the internationals have forgotten what we went through, not just for the last two years but for centuries. Always we have been betrayed by the Europeans—at the Congress of Berlin in 1878, and in London in 1913, where Albanian land was divided…. The Serbs will return eventually because their homes are here. If they were not involved in crime—then why not? They should accept themselves as a minority in Kosova. But Albanians can never be familiar with them. In Gjakovë only 2 percent of the inhabitants were Serbs, and they were close to many Albanians, often godfathers to Albanian children—and that's why people are so angry here. Once again, the Serbs have betrayed us.

Fatime Boshnjaku, Albanian, age 50
Gjakovë (Djakovica), February 20, 2001

My mother is Bosniak, and my father is Albanian. My mother graduated as a philologist and is a correspondent for Japanese TV. My father used to be a music teacher and clarinetist. I had private piano lessons before the war—in our illegal Albanian education system. Now, I'm back in a normal high school and will graduate this summer. My Bosniak friends have all gone to Bosnia. They didn't speak Albanian and used to socialize with Serbs. I see them when I visit Sarajevo; they miss Kosova a lot.

After we fled Prishtina, we stayed in a private house in Macedonia. We went to a disco in Gostivar once a week to forget the war and let off steam. I was very bored there. We couldn't wear sleeveless shirts because all the women were covered.* The locals criticized us: "We feel sorry for you, and then you go out dancing!" I said, "If we don't go out, we'll go crazy."

In the evenings, I played piano in a school in Tetovë—the *Toccata* by Khachaturian, the easier Mozart sonatas, Chopin's *Nocturne*, and Bach's *Prelude and Fugue*. I'd cry every time I played, because I missed my teacher. I felt so sad leaving my piano in Prishtina. My friends in Macedonia were violinists, clarinetists, and flautists who all brought their instruments with them across the border. If we were upset, we let it all out by playing. Music was like food for us. It gave us strength and helped us forget the war.

My dad remained in Prishtina. We did not hear from him for six weeks. Finally, we got through to our Serb neighbor, Duška, on the phone, and she fetched my dad to speak to us. She helped a lot. She bought my dad bread two or three times because it was too dangerous for him to leave the flat. But she was scared because the Serbs would have killed her if they had seen her helping him. Other neighbors told me that Duška's husband used to maltreat Albanians. Her son was a soldier who was killed in the war by Albanians before NATO's arrival. As soon as NATO came, she and her husband left for Belgrade. At the time, I was not sorry she left, but my attitude has changed a lot in the past eighteen months. At first, I thought only Serbs were bad, but then I realized there are bad people everywhere, including bad Albanians. I was disappointed in the behavior of the Albanians after the war. When they killed the Bulgarian UN guy because he replied to their question in Serbian,** I felt ashamed to be Albanian. A language is a language, and if the language is Serbian, that's not important. If someone is a good person, who cares if he is Serb or not? No country in the world is ethnically clean. For me, it's not important if a person is Rom, or whatever, as longer as that person is good, civilized. Even

if both my parents were Albanian, I would have the same attitude. Right after the war, I didn't speak out when my friends criticized the Serbs, but now I cannot hold it in. There is only a small minority who think like me. My friends joke around, saying, "She's a Bosniak!"—not with hostility but understanding that I'm more tolerant.

Yesterday, I wanted to vote, but I wasn't allowed because I'm not yet eighteen. It was very exciting. I was pleased that the Albanians behaved so well and showed they were civilized. It was the quietest day since the war. I would have voted LDK because this party has existed for ten years, whereas the PDK only started up after the war. My best friend supports Ramush Haradinaj, so we get into big arguments—and then hug each other and say it'll be good whatever happens. Whoever wins, it's a victory for the Albanians. Whoever wins, the internationals will rule, they're in control.

Linda Kllokoqi, age 17, Albanian/Bosniak
Prishtina (Priština), October 29, 2000

* The Albanians of Tetovo, Macedonia are generally more religious than their counterparts in Kosovo.

** Valentin Krumov was a U.S. citizen of Bulgarian descent who came to Kosovo from New York to work for the UN. He had just arrived, when he was murdered by Albanian youths on October 11, 1999, because he gave them the time in Serbian.

Back in the early 1980s, I used to drink coffee with the Serbian police. I would ask them, "What do you think? Can we live together?" They would say we couldn't. Later, in the early 1990s, the Serbian police chief visited me here and was courteous to me, talking to me in Albanian and using old Kosovar sayings such as, "The water goes and the sand stays," and "What goes around, comes around." He meant that the regime may change, but the people stay the same; and even if the Serbs have to leave Kosova, they will be back one day. A few days after your visit in 1995, the police chief came here again. This time he asked questions about you—who were you? where were you from? I said you were just a guest from London.

Then, in 1998, some one hundred policemen surrounded our house. The police chief went into the *oda*, and shouted at me, "Where is your rifle? Why didn't you hand it in?" Another policeman said, "You are saving it to kill Serbs!" and pointed his gun at me. I had to give up my hunting gun, which my father had given me when I was born. They also accused me of being a KLA Commander, but when I denied it, they believed me—they know that in our culture, old people don't lie. It's not good to lie when you are close to death.

In 1999, both my sons joined the KLA, and later I, too, fought with them when we were under attack near my home village. I was the oldest in our group. The younger KLA men respected me and looked up to me as if I were their father. It was the first time I'd fought since I had been a conscript in Tito's time, in the mid 1950s, but I remembered all my army training. On June 7, 1999, I came back here with my family. The police had moved into my house, and they threatened to burn it because my sons were in the KLA. They told me to go to Albania or Macedonia, but I refused. I love Kosova; I was born here and I will die here. I had to give them DM 1000 to save the house from being burned.

A few days later, I heard my neighbor shooting into the air. NATO had arrived! My son came down from the mountains in his KLA uniform. We were so happy. Everyone went out with flowers, and the KFOR soldiers gave us biscuits and sweets; the kids were hugging the soldiers. I'm an optimist, so I'd always expected NATO would come. I see the KFOR soldiers as my sons. I feel this freedom as sweet as honey: my heart is melting with happiness like sugar. I've never been to school—not a single day—but I know there is a God and I love my faith.

During the war, the Serbs in Banjskë, the village across the road, always protected the

Albanians. Two villages nearby had been destroyed, but Banjskë was spared. The Serbs said, "We'll look after you," and the Albanians said, "We'll take care of you, but if the KLA comes, we aren't responsible." The KLA did come, but when they heard this story, they didn't harm the Serbs. The Serb police have left Banjskë now; there are only honest civilians there.

The other day, I greeted a Serb neighbor, and he said in Albanian, "How are you?" My son nearly slapped me because I was talking to a Serb. Of course, my sons don't like the Serbs—so many of their friends have been killed. But I don't feel hatred for those who didn't do anything, the Serbs who were born here and lived here all their lives. I'm a Muslim, so I must be sympathetic. I love every man who keeps his faith, Catholic or Muslim. He who is religious, loves the world. But my sons are not religious. The young Serbs don't know about God, and if you don't know God exists, you don't like other people.

Of course, we can live with the Serbs again. There have been many wars between us, and both before and after the wars, we would sit together and eat together. I would never turn away a hungry guest from my house, even a Serb.

If KFOR leaves, war will break out again. Albanians do not want to be in a confederation with Serbia, because it was so bad when the Serbs were in control here. I hope we can settle things with dialogue. I believe Kosova will be independent, but maybe not within my lifetime.

Ali Hyseni, age 74, Albanian
Ugmir (Dobra Luka), September 26, 1999, April 29, 2000, and October 15, 2000

KOSOVO

Albanian spelling	Serbian spelling
Banjskë	Banjska
Celinë	Celina
Deçan	Dečani
Dragash	Dragaš
Fushë Kosovë	Kosovo Polje
Gjakovë	Djakovica
Gllogovc	Glogovac
Gorazhdec	Goraždevac
Graçkë	Gračko
Jabllanicë	Jablanica
Koliq	Kolić
Koshtanjevë	Koshtandjeva
Lipjan	Lipljan
Llapla Sellë	Laplje Selo
Lluzhan	Lužane
Lubizhde	Ljubiżda
Makovc	Makovce
Mitrovicë	Kosovska Mitrovica
Obiliq	Obilić
Orllan	Orlane
Pejë	Peć
Plemetin	Plementina
Podujevë	Podujevo
Prishtina/Prishtinë	Priština
Prizren	Prizren
Prugovc	Prugovce
Rahovec	Orahovac

KOSOVO

Albanian spelling	Serbian spelling
Reçak	Račak
Sekiraçë	Sekirača
Shajkovc	Šajkovce
Trepça	Trepča
Ugmir	Dobra Luka
Ulkian/Graçanicë	Gračanica
Vërbovc	Verbovac
Vushtrri	Vučitrn
Zhupa (valley)	Župa

MACEDONIA

Macedonian	Albanian
Čegrane	Çegranë
Neprošteno	Neproshten
Stenkovec	Stankovec
Tetovo	Tetovë

SERBIA

Serbian	Albanian
Medvedja	Medvegja
Niš	Nish
Prokuplje	Prokuple

Alliance for Kosova's Future (AAK). *See* **elections**.

ar: Measure of land ten meters by ten meters (Serbian).

Arkan, a.k.a. Željko Ražnatović. Arkan's Tigers were feared for their extreme brutality and efficiency. They were known as the paramilitary shock troops of the "ethnic cleansing" operations in Croatia, Bosnia and Kosovo. Arkan was assassinated in Belgrade on January 15, 2000.

Ashkalia. Members of the Roma community who speak Albanian. The Ashkalia were partly integrated into the Kosova Albanian community before the war.

Bajram. Feast of Sacrifice, one of greatest feast days in the Muslim calendar.

Bosniaks. Muslim Slavs speaking the Bosnian language.

Democratic League of Kosova (LDK). *See* **elections**.

Democratic Party of Kosova (PDK). *See* **elections**.

elections. Local elections were held in Kosovo on October 28, 2000. The Democratic League of Kosova (LDK), led by Dr. Ibrahim Rugova, gained 58 percent. The Democratic Party of Kosova (PDK), led by ex-KLA chief Hashim Thaçi, gained 28 percent, and the Alliance for Kosova's Future (AAK) led by ex- KLA officer Ramush Haradinaj, 8 percent. There was an 80 percent turn out of the Albanian majority in the province.

Goranis. Inhabitants of the mountainous region (Gora) near the borders of Macedonia and Albania. Most members of the Gorani community consider themselves Muslim Slavs.

Haradinaj, Ramush. Leader of AAK. *See also* **elections**.

ICTY. International Criminal Tribunal for the former Yugoslavia, based in The Hague.

Illyrians. Believed by many to be the ancestors of today's Albanians.

Imam. Leader of congregational prayer in a mosque.

Ishalla. God willing (Albanian).

KFOR. NATO-led peacekeeping force in Kosovo.

Kosovo A and **Kosovo B**. Power stations in Obiliq (Obilić) near Prishtina.

KLA. Kosova Liberation Army.

LDK. Democratic League of Kosovo. See also **elections**.

Milošević, Slobodan. Former President of Yugoslavia, ousted in 2000.

Motrat Qiriazi. The Qiriazi Sisters, an Albanian rural women's group. Motrat Qiriazi helped train Roma, Ashkali and Egyptian women (at their request) to run their own women's network.

NATO. North Atlantic Treaty Organization.

NGO. Non-governmental organization.

oda. Room for receiving and entertaining guests.

OSCE. Organization for Security and Cooperation in Europe.

PDK. Democratic Party of Kosova. See also **elections**.

Ramadan. The ninth month of the Muslim lunar calendar, and also the Muslim month of fasting. The month of Ramadan ends with one of the great feast days of the Muslim calendar, Eid Al-Fittr.

Roma. Gypsies, mostly living in eastern Europe.

Rugova, Ibrahim. *See* **elections**.

SFOR. NATO Stabilization Force based in Bosnia.

Skënderbeg, Gjergj Kastrioti Skënderbeg. Born 1405, a prominent leader in the Balkan countries' struggle against Ottoman Turkish domination. He is considered a national hero by the Albanians.

King Stefan. Probably Stefan Dušan, 1331-1355.

Thaçi, Hashim. *See* **elections**.

"The Hague tribunal." *See* **ICTY**.

Turkish Red Crescent. A charity/aid agency partly supported by the Turkish government and affiliated with the International Red Cross.

UÇK. Ushtria Çlirimtare e Kosovës, Albanian for Kosova Liberation Army.

UNHCR. United Nations High Commissioner for Refugees.

UNMIK. United Nations Mission (Administration) in Kosovo.

VJ. Vojska Jugoslavije, Yugoslav Army.

Women In Black Against War. Žene u Crnom protiv Rata, Belgrade-based feminist protest group, demonstrated regularly in the 1990s in silent vigils against the nationalism and war-orientation of the Milošević regime. Women in Black is an international peace network.

YU Programme Building. Apartment block in Prishtina under KFOR protection inhabited by Serbs and internationals.